YORK NOTES

General Editors: Professor A.N.Jeffares (*University of Stirling*) & Professor Suheil Bushrui (*American University of Beirut*)

Anton Chekhov

THE CHERRY ORCHARD

Notes by Helena Forsås-Scott

FILOSOFIE MAGISTER (GOTHENBURG) PH D (ABERDEEN)

LONGMAN
YORK PRESS

YORK PRESS
Immeuble Esseily, Place Riad Solh, Beirut.

LONGMAN GROUP LIMITED
Longman House,
Burnt Mill,
Harlow,
Essex.

First published 1983
ISBN 0 582 79220 7
Printed in Hong Kong by
Wilture Enterprises (International) Ltd.

Contents

Part 1

Introduction

The author

Anton Pavlovich Chekhov was born in 1860 in the small Russian town of Taganrog, which is situated on the Sea of Azov, to the north of the Black Sea. His father, who was a shopkeeper, went bankrupt when Anton was in his teens. The family then moved to Moscow, with Anton staying behind in Taganrog to complete his schooling.

In 1879, Chekhov enrolled as a medical student at Moscow University. In the following year, he had his first piece published, in a St Petersburg magazine, and over the next few years he established himself as a writer of sketches and humorous tales. Initially, Chekhov had no great literary aspirations, but wrote for the sake of the money: his large family was still poor and depended on him for financial support.

By 1884, when Chekhov's first book of stories appeared, he had had hundreds of pieces published in various magazines. In the same year, he qualified as a doctor. He practised as a doctor throughout much of his life, and his scientific training and medical experience came to exert a significant influence both on his outlook and on his writing.

During the second half of the 1880s, Chekhov published further volumes of stories, contributed to magazines and newspapers, and had his first plays performed. He had been interested in the theatre since he was a schoolboy, and over the years he had tried his hand at playwriting on several occasions. Thus, in the early 1880s, he had spent a long time working on a full-length play, only to destroy the manuscript when the play was rejected by a Moscow theatre. The four-act play *Ivanov* was written in the autumn of 1887 and staged the same year, causing uproar among the audience and receiving mixed reviews. A revised version of *Ivanov*, performed early in 1889, got a better reception. By then, Chekhov had enjoyed a huge theatrical success with a one-act play, *The Bear*, which, towards the end of 1888, was running at several theatres simultaneously. *The Bear* was followed by further one-act plays, among them *The Proposal*.

In 1890 Chekhov turned his back on Moscow, embarking, in spring, on a long and hazardous journey which was to take up most of the remainder of the year. Traversing Siberia, he went to the island of Sakhalin, a Russian penal colony. He spent several months on the island, interviewing its population and collecting material for an extensive report. He returned to Moscow via Hong Kong, Singapore, Ceylon, and Odessa. His *Sakhalin Island* was published in 1893–4.

Having visited Europe in the spring of 1891, Chekhov moved to an estate outside Moscow in the following year. He continued to write stories as well as plays. In October 1896 a St Petersburg theatre staged *The Seagull*, a play written during the previous year. The performance was a disaster, and Chekhov assured a friend that 'I shall *never* either write plays or have them acted.'*

Early in 1897 there was a serious deterioration in Chekhov's health. Having shown the first symptoms of tuberculosis in the mid-1880s, Chekhov now suffered a haemorrhage of the lungs. After spending some time in a Moscow clinic he travelled to Europe, where he spent the following winter convalescing in the south of France.

In 1898, *The Seagull* was taken up by the newly established Moscow Art Theatre. In this production, the play became a great success, marking Chekhov's breakthrough as a serious playwright. It also marked the beginning of his close association with the Moscow Art Theatre, which was to last until the end of his life.

For health reasons, Chekhov spent the winter of 1898–9 in the Crimea, and in 1899 went to live permanently in Yalta. In the same year, his play *Uncle Vanya* was performed by the Moscow Art Theatre. *Uncle Vanya* was based on an earlier play, *The Wood Demon*, which had been a failure when it was first performed in 1889; Chekhov had since revised it, but although the play had appeared in print in 1897, it was another two years before he consented to having it performed. He saw the play for the first time in 1900, when the Moscow Art Theatre visited the Crimea.

Three Sisters, written in 1900, was performed by the Moscow Art Theatre in the following year, with the actress Olga Knipper playing the role of Masha. Chekhov by then had known Olga Knipper for some years, and in May 1901 they were married. While Olga Knipper continued her career as an actress in Moscow, Chekhov was forced by his failing health to spend most of his time in Yalta. He continued to write stories and also worked on the complete edition of his works. Much of the spring and early summer of 1902 he devoted to nursing his sick wife, who had suffered a miscarriage in March.

With his own deteriorating state of health making work increasingly difficult, Chekhov spent part of 1902 and much of 1903 on what was to become his last play, *The Cherry Orchard*. The Moscow Art Theatre began rehearsing it in the autumn of 1903, and it received its first performance in January 1904. On the same occasion, a Chekhov jubilee

*Letter to A. S. Souvorin, 18 October 1896, in *Letters on the Short Story, the Drama and other Literary Topics by Anton Chekhov*, selected and edited by Louis S. Friedland, Vision Press, London, 1965, p. 147.

was arranged, with the ailing author appearing on the stage between Acts 3 and 4, to be greeted with flowers and speeches.

In June 1904 Chekhov and his wife set out on a journey to Europe. He died at Badenweiler in the Black Forest in Germany on 2 July 1904.

Chekhov's Russia

The birth of Anton Chekhov coincided with a period that has become known in Russian history as the 'age of the great reforms'.* Tsar Alexander II, who reigned from 1855 to 1881, began his spell in office with a decade of unprecedented liberalisation. Most important among the reforms was the abolition of serfdom in 1861. Chekhov's father had been born a serf, but Chekhov's grandfather had succeeded in saving enough money to buy the freedom of his family and himself in 1841. Another reform concerned the reorganisation of local government, in which a large measure of self-government was introduced. A new administrative unit, the *zemstvo*, was established and given a wide range of responsibilities, among them the provision of health care and primary education. Chekhov was directly involved in both these areas, doing much medical work as a *zemstvo* doctor, and initiating the building of several rural schools. His remarkable journey to the penal colony on the island of Sakhalin and his extensive report on conditions there similarly reflect his practical concern with humanitarian issues.

But the 'age of the great reforms' soon came to an end: after an attempt on the Tsar's life in 1866, a period of reaction set in. When the Tsar was eventually assassinated in 1881, he was succeeded by Alexander III, whose regime was one of extreme reaction. Nevertheless, social and economic changes were continuing to transform the country. The aristocracy's grip on the economy was beginning to slacken: without recourse to serfs, many aristocrats were finding the management of their rural estates increasingly difficult, and some of them were perpetually in debt. But a new class of merchants and businessmen was appearing, sustained by the growth of industry and the improvements in communications. These changes are reflected in Chekhov's works, not least in *The Cherry Orchard*.

Chekhov's ideas and Chekhov's theatre

Not surprisingly, the artist and doctor who was a descendant of serfs regarded freedom as a key concept. And inevitably, Chekhov's demands went far beyond mere physical freedom. 'My holy of holies', he wrote in 1889, 'is the human body, health, intelligence, talent, inspiration, love,

*W. H. Bruford, *Chekhov and his Russia: A Sociological Study*, Kegan Paul, Trench, Trubner & Co., London, 1947, p. 32.

and the most absolute freedom – freedom from violence and lying, whatever forms they take. This is the program I would follow if I were a great artist.'*

As Chekhov was well aware, the problems of putting a programme of this kind into practice were immense, not least for a writer of his own background. The mentality of the slave was not abolished by a mere change in the law. In a letter written early in 1889, Chekhov illustrates this point in terms which are obviously relevant to his own situation:

> What writers belonging to the upper class have received from nature for nothing, plebeians acquire at the cost of their youth. Write a story of how a young man, the son of a serf who has served in a shop, sung in a choir, been at a high school and a university, who has been brought up to respect everyone of higher rank and position, to kiss priests' hands, to reverence other people's ideas, to be thankful for every morsel of bread, who has been many times whipped, who has trudged from one pupil to another without goloshes, who has been used to fighting and to tormenting animals, who has liked dining with his rich relatives, and been hypocritical before God and men from the mere consciousness of his own insignificance – write how this young man squeezes the slave out of himself, drop by drop, and how waking one beautiful morning he feels that he has no longer a slave's blood in his veins but a real man's.†

Chekhov's acute awareness of the significance of human dignity imbues all his writing. Characteristic is his reaction, at the age of sixteen, to a letter in which his younger brother, Mikhail, had signed himself 'your worthless and insignificant brother'. 'You recognize your insignificance?', Chekhov wrote. 'Recognize it before God; perhaps, too, in the presence of beauty, wisdom, nature, but not before men. Among men you must be conscious of your dignity and worth . . . . Respect yourself as an honest man and know that an honest man is not something worthless.'‡

In Chekhov's opinion, the chief task of the artist was the unveiling of truth. 'Artistic literature', he wrote in 1887, 'is called so just because it depicts life as it really is. Its aim is truth, – unconditional and honest.' 'A writer', he continued, 'must be as objective as a chemist: he must abandon the subjective line; he must know that dung-heaps play a very respectable part in a landscape, and that evil passions are as inherent in life as good ones.'§

Chekhov's artistic concern with truthfulness and his all-pervading

---

*Letter to A. N. Pleshcheyev, October 1889, in *Letters*, ed. Friedland, p. 63.
†Letter to A. S. Souvorin, 7 January 1889, in *Letters*, ed. Friedland, pp. 100–1.
‡Letter to Mikhail P. Chekhov, 1 July 1876, in *Letters*, ed. Friedland, p. 291.
§Letter to M. V. Kiselev, 14 January 1887, in *Letters*, ed. Friedland, pp. 275–6.

respect for human dignity both underlie his conviction that it is the duty of the artist not to solve problems but to state problems correctly. In his opinion, 'the artist should be, not the judge of his characters and their conversations, but only an unbiassed witness.' And Chekhov went on to illustrate his thesis: 'I once overheard a desultory conversation about pessimism between two Russians; nothing was solved, – and my business is to report the conversation exactly as I heard it, and let the jury, – that is, the readers, estimate its value.' To Chekhov's way of thinking, the absence of a solution was no admission of defeat on the part of the artist; on the contrary, he argued that the artist who dared admit that he did not understand anything was making a direct contribution to progress:

> The mob think they know and understand everything; the more stupid they are, the wider, I think, do they conceive their horizon to be. And if an artist in whom the crowd has faith decides to declare that he understands nothing of what he sees, – this in itself constitutes a considerable clarity in the realm of thought, and a great step forward.*

As a writer of fiction, Chekhov could enjoy full freedom to implement his ideas about artistic truthfulness and honesty. As a playwright, by contrast, he had to depend on existing conventions of acting and production. And the theatre for which Chekhov wrote his first plays in the 1880s was dominated by pomposity and exaggeration, by thoughtless conventionality of production and by star acting.

Not surprisingly, Chekhov was ruthless in his criticism of any kind of falsity on the stage. Famous are his comments on the great French actress Sarah Bernhardt, who spellbound the Moscow audiences on her visit in 1881; Chekhov, however, found that her every sigh, 'her tears, her death agonies, all her acting – is nothing other than a lesson cleverly and faultlessly learned by heart'. 'There were moments in her acting which touched us almost to tears', he wrote; 'but the tears did not flow because all the charm was effaced by artificiality.'†

An instructive illustration of Chekhov's ideas about acting is to be found in a letter to Olga Knipper, in which he sets out his concept of how to present a nervous man on the stage. Most people, Chekhov reminds the actress, are in fact nervous:

> the greater number suffer, and a small proportion feel acute pain; but where – in streets and in houses – do you see people tearing about, leaping up, and clutching at their heads? Suffering ought to be expressed as it is expressed in life – that is, not by the arms and legs,

*Letter to A. S. Souvorin, 30 May 1888, in *Letters*, ed. Friedland, pp. 58–9.
†Ernest J. Simmons, *Chekhov: A Biography*, Cape, London, 1963, p. 49.

but by the tone and expression; not by gesticulation, but by grace. Subtle emotions of the soul in educated people must be subtly expressed in an external way. You will say – stage conditions. No conditions allow falsity.*

The demands for truth and realism were central to naturalistic drama. Inspired by an essay by the French writer Emile Zola (1840–1902), 'Naturalism on the Stage' (1881), naturalistic drama spread quickly through Europe, its main exponents being playwrights such as August Strindberg in Sweden, Henrik Ibsen in Norway, and Gerhardt Hauptmann in Germany. Among the leading naturalistic theatres were Antoine's Théâtre Libre in Paris and Otto Brahm's Freie Bühne in Berlin. In Russia, naturalistic ideas were taken up and developed by Konstantin Stanislavsky (1863–1938), an actor and producer, who founded the Moscow Art Theatre in 1898. 'Our program', Stanislavsky later explained, 'was revolutionary; we rebelled against the old way of acting, against affectation, and false pathos, against declamation and bohemian exaggeration, against bad conventionality of production and sets, against the star system which ruined the ensemble.'†

Defying the star system, which meant that whole productions were designed around the star actors, Stanislavsky instead placed the emphasis on the play as a work of art. Conceived by the playwright as an artistic entity, the play, he argued, had to be produced in a way which would do justice to its aesthetic coherence. From his actors he demanded meticulous attention to the text of the play, great sensitivity to mood and atmosphere, total honesty and sincerity in their interpretation of their parts, and the strictest discipline, in both rehearsal and performance.

One of the Moscow Art Theatre's first great successes was Chekhov's *The Seagull*, which had failed so miserably in its original St Petersburg production. To mark the significance of this success, a seagull became the emblem of the Moscow Art Theatre. A close relationship was established with Chekhov, whose subsequent plays all received their first performance at the Moscow Art Theatre. There can be no doubt that this relationship between playwright and theatre was mutually beneficial. Chekhov, however, sometimes had reason to disagree with Stanislavsky's interpretations of his plays. His most consistent complaint concerned Stanislavsky's ideas about naturalism on the stage, which often went far beyond anything that he himself had had in mind. An illuminating tale, which brings out Chekhov's scrupulous respect for the integrity of the work of art, is told by Vsevolod Meyerhold, the actor and theatre director. Meyerhold describes how at a

*Letter to O. L. Knipper, 2 January 1900, in *Letters*, ed. Friedland, p. 186.
†Marc Slonim, *Russian Theater from the Empire to the Soviets*, Methuen, London, 1963, p. 109.

rehearsal of *The Seagull* one of the actors told Chehkov that Stanislavsky had introduced a number of additional sound effects, so that

> during the play, frogs croaked backstage, dragonflies hummed, and dogs howled.
> 'What for?' asked Anton Pavlovich, sounding dissatisfied.
> 'It's realistic,' said the actor.
> 'Realistic,' A. P. repeated with a laugh. And then after a brief pause, he remarked: 'The stage is art. In one of [I. N.] Kramskoy's genre paintings he has some magnificently drawn faces. What if we cut the painted nose from one of these faces and substituted a live one? The new nose would be "real," but the painting would be ruined.'*

A note on the text

The first English translation of *The Cherry Orchard* was published in 1908, and many different translations have appeared since then. One of the best-known early translations is the one by Constance Garnett: *The Plays of Tchehov*, 2 vols., Chatto & Windus, London, 1923 (the translation of *The Cherry Orchard* is printed in Volume I). Garnett's language has a distinctive period flavour, which is why a modern critic such as J. L. Styan prefers this translation to more recent ones.

A translation by S. S. Koteliansky is available in the Everyman Library Edition: *Plays and Stories*, Dent, London. The Everyman volume was first published in 1937, and apart from *The Cherry Orchard*, it contains some other plays by Chekhov and a number of stories.

The translation used in these Notes is that of Elisaveta Fen, published in the Penguin Classics Series: Chekhov, *Plays*, Penguin Books, Harmondsworth, 1959. Fen's translation of the play first appeared in 1951. As well as *The Cherry Orchard*, the Penguin volume contains four other full-length plays and three one-act plays. The texts are prefaced by an extensive introduction, written by the translator.

A more recent translation of the play is that of Ronald Hingley, published in Volume III of *The Oxford Chekhov*, Oxford University Press, London, 1964. Hingley's volume contains a general introduction, but particularly useful are the appendices which accompany each of the plays. In these the translator has gathered Chekhov's comments on the plays, arranging the material under headings such as 'The composition', 'The text', and 'Some further comments by Chekhov'. In Hingley's volume are also included notes on words and phrases, details about the pronunciation of Russian names, and a bibliography. The overall tone of Hingley's translation differs noticeably from Fen's, and a comparison between the two may result in some fresh perspectives on the play.

*V. Meyerhold, 'Naturalistic theater and theater of mood', in *Chekhov. A Collection of Critical Essays*, ed. R. L. Jackson, Prentice-Hall, Englewood Cliffs, N.J., 1967, pp. 65–6.

Part 2

Summaries
of THE CHERRY ORCHARD

A general summary

In the nursery on Liubov Andryeevna's estate, Lopakhin, a business-man, and Dooniasha, a parlourmaid, are waiting up for the owner, who is about to return after five years abroad. Liubov soon arrives, bringing with her Ania, her daughter, Varia, her adopted daughter, and Charlotta, a governess. They are accompanied by Gayev, who is Liubov's brother, and by Simeonov-Pishchik, a landowner.

Varia reveals to Ania, who has accompanied Liubov abroad, that they have not succeeded in paying the interest on their debts; as a result, the estate will be up for sale in a few months' time. She also explains that although everybody is expecting her to marry Lopakhin, he has not yet proposed to her. Varia herself would most of all like to become a nun.

Feers, the aged man-servant, prepares coffee for Liubov, Gayev, Lopakhin, and Simeonov-Pishchik. Lopakhin presents his plan for saving the estate: the cherry orchard should be cut down and the land divided into plots for summer residences for people from the near-by town. The rent would bring in more than enough money to pay off the family's debts. Liubov and Gayev are outraged by Lopakhin's plan.

When Lopakhin has left, Liubov and Gayev turn to admiring the orchard, which is in blossom. Liubov speaks of her happy childhood. But the arrival of Trofimov, who used to be the tutor of her dead son, makes her weep.

Pishchik takes his leave, but only after having made Liubov promise to lend him some money: he is always in debt.

When Varia and Gayev are alone, they discuss various plans for saving the estate. Gayev strikes an optimistic note: their rich aunt might help them, or they could marry Ania off to some wealthy man, or they could try to arrange a loan. Varia is sceptical, but Ania, who has suddenly appeared, believes in her uncle's assurances. As the act closes, Trofimov crosses the stage. His behaviour suggests that he is in love with Ania.

Act 2 is set in the open country. By the roadside are an old shrine, a well, a seat, and some ancient gravestones. The outlines of a large town can be seen on the horizon.

Charlotta, who has brought a shot-gun, speaks of her childhood and her loneliness, while Yepihodov, the clerk who is in love with

Dooniasha, sings and plays the guitar. When Yepihodov asks to speak to Dooniasha, she finds an excuse for sending him away, and in the meantime she declares her love for Yasha, Liubov's young servant. Yasha seems indifferent.

Liubov, Gayev, and Lopakhin find Yasha alone by the shrine. Lopakhin is angered by Liubov's and Gayev's attitude to his plan for saving the estate. Liubov speaks of how she has always squandered money. Her husband, a heavy drinker, was always in debt, and when she went abroad after the deaths of her husband and her son, it was only to land herself in debt again, after three years of caring for her sick lover in France. She tears up another telegram which she has just received from her lover.

A band is heard playing in the distance, and Liubov suggests that the musicians be invited to the estate and they all have a dance. Criticising Lopakhin for leading a drab life, Liubov advises him to marry Varia.

Trofimov, Ania, and Varia arrive. Trofimov and Lopakhin argue, Trofimov asserting that mankind is always advancing and that a better future is lying ahead, but Lopakhin is less optimistic: he has been saddened to find just how few honest and decent people there are about.

Inspired by the setting of the sun, Gayev starts making an emotional speech to nature, but he is quickly stopped by Ania, Varia, and Trofimov. They all sit in silence. Then a sound is heard, like that of a string snapping. They are all startled by the sound and try to explain it in a variety of ways.

A tramp appears, asks the way to the station, and begs money from Varia. Liubov gives him a gold coin. This angers Varia, as there is no food in the house, but Liubov makes Lopakhin promise to lend her money. Liubov tells Varia that they have almost fixed up her marriage to Lopakhin.

Trofimov and Ania are left alone. Trofimov asserts that they are above falling in love; all that matters now is humanity's march forward. He points out that Ania and her family are living in debt to the serfs whom they have owned for generations, and that in order to start living in the present they shall have to atone for the past. Inspired by Ania's admiration, Trofimov waxes lyrical about the future. Eventually, they walk down towards the river in the moonlight, while Varia can be heard calling for her sister.

Act 3 is set in the drawing-room of the house. In the ballroom, which can be seen through an archway at the back, people are dancing.

Pishchik and Trofimov come into the drawing-room. Trofimov criticises Pishchik for always being in debt, and Pishchik searches all his pockets for the money he is due to pay in two days' time. Liubov enters, worrying about her brother, who is late after having gone to town for the auction of the estate. Charlotta astonishes Pishchik with her tricks, first with cards, then as a ventriloquist, and, finally, as an auctioneer.

Liubov again brings up her worries about her brother, this time with Varia. She also tells Varia that she ought to marry Lopakhin; but Varia is convinced that Lopakhin's sole interest is his business.

Left alone with Trofimov, Liubov speaks of her anxiety, only to be told that she must look the truth straight in the face. Liubov argues that Trofimov's inexperience of life is making all problems appear simple to him. Her lover, who is ill, is asking her to return to Paris, and Liubov knows that she will be doing so, for she loves him. Trofimov retorts that Liubov's lover has been robbing her of her money. This angers Liubov, who thinks that Trofimov ought to have some understanding of people who are in love; indeed, she says, at his age he is daft not to have a mistress. Horrified, Trofimov leaves. The sound is heard of someone running up the stairs and then falling down with a crash. Ania runs in, laughing, to report that Trofimov has fallen down the stairs.

The station-master starts reciting a poem but is interrupted by the band striking up a waltz. Liubov and Trofimov dance.

Feers tells Yasha about the balls they used to have in the past. He is full of contempt for the kind of guests they are having to invite nowadays.

Liubov is told by Ania that a man in the kitchen has reported that the cherry orchard has been sold, but nobody knows to whom.

Liubov wonders where Feers will go if the estate is sold, and he replies that he will go wherever she orders him. Thinking that Feers looks unwell, Liubov tells him to go to bed, but he points out that if he did, there would be nobody to wait on the guests. Yasha attempts to make Liubov promise that if she goes to Paris, she will take him with her.

Dooniasha tells Feers about the compliment she has been paid by the post-office clerk. Yepihodov, noticing Dooniasha's elation, complains about his misfortunes.

Varia is annoyed to find Yepihodov in the drawing-room, orders him out, and threatens him with Feers's stick. Lopakhin enters. The auction, he explains, was over by four o'clock, but he and Gayev missed the train. Gayev enters, claiming to be hungry and tired – but then he is off to play billiards. Eventually, Lopakhin confirms that the orchard has been sold, and that he has bought it.

Liubov is overcome with emotion. Varia throws the keys of the house on the floor and walks out.

Describing the auction, Lopakhin wishes that his father and grandfather could have witnessed his triumph: he has bought the estate where they were serfs.

The band starts playing again. Liubov is crying and Lopakhin tries to comfort her. He leaves the room in the company of Pishchik, speaking ironically of himself as the new landowner.

Ania kneels beside her mother, reminding her that she still has her life ahead of her. Ania promises Liubov that they will plant a new cherry orchard, even more splendid than the one which has just been sold.

Act 4 is again set in the nursery. Now it is virtually empty. Furniture has been piled up in a corner, and suitcases and other items of luggage are waiting by the door.

Lopakhin and Yasha are in the nursery. Yasha is holding a tray with glasses of champagne. When Liubov and Gayev enter, Lopakhin offers them champagne, but they refuse. Yasha liberally helps himself.

Trofimov enters, unable to find his goloshes. He, too, refuses a drink. He also turns down Lopakhin's offer of money, and again speaks of his faith in the future.

The sound of an axe striking a tree is heard from outside. Ania asks Lopakhin not to start cutting down the orchard until Liubov has left.

Ania turns to Yasha: she wants to know if Feers has been taken to hospital. Yasha believes that he has.

Dooniasha tries to persuade Yasha not to leave her behind, but Yasha appears as indifferent to her arguments as he is to Dooniasha herself.

Liubov enters together with Gayev, Ania, and Charlotta. Liubov says goodbye to the house, which is due to be pulled down the following spring. She herself will be going to Paris, while Ania is to stay behind to attend the high school.

Charlotta again performs some tricks. She tells Lopakhin that she will have nowhere to live once she has left the estate.

Pishchik arrives. Unexpectedly, he has made some money, and now he is wanting to pay some of his debts to Lopakhin and Liubov. Only when leaving does he realise that the family is moving out of the house.

Asking about Feers, Liubov is assured that he has been taken to hospital. She again brings up the subject of Varia's future, and Lopakhin suggests that they arrange the details about the marriage immediately. But the few minutes which Lopakhin spends with Varia are taken up with trivial comments about their various plans for the future and about the weather, and Lopakhin leaves without having made his proposal.

Gayev starts making a farewell speech, but Ania and Varia stop him.

Lopakhin begins to lock the doors. Liubov and Gayev embrace. The stage is empty.

There is a sequence of sounds as doors are being locked and carriages driven away. An axe thuds against a tree in the orchard.

Feers enters, looking ill. He tries one of the doors and realises that it is locked. He sits down on a sofa, muttering. He lies down and remains motionless.

A sound, like that of a string snapping, is heard. It is followed by silence. Again, an axe strikes a tree in the orchard.

Detailed summaries

Act 1

The opening act of *The Cherry Orchard* is set in a room in Liubov Andryeevna's house which is still known as the nursery. It is a very early morning in May, and the sun is rising. The cherry trees, which are in blossom, can be seen through the windows. But the night has been cold, with a frost.

Dooniasha, a parlourmaid, and Lopakhin, a businessman, are waiting up for Liubov Andryeevna, who is returning to her estate after having spent five years abroad. Lopakhin has been intending to meet her at the station, and is annoyed that he has overslept. He recalls Liubov's kindness to him when, as a child, he had been beaten by his father. On that occasion, Liubov called him 'little peasant', and Lopakhin reflects that although he is now rich and well dressed, he still remains a peasant beneath the surface. As if to confirm his assertion, he observes that he has not understood a word of the book he has been trying to read; indeed, he has fallen asleep over it.

Dooniasha is tense and agitated as she awaits Liubov's arrival. Lopakhin criticises the parlourmaid for behaving and dressing like a lady: she should remember her proper place.

Yepihodov, a clerk on the estate, arrives with a bunch of flowers, which he promptly drops on the floor. Complaining about his squeaky boots, he tells Lopakhin that something unpleasant seems to happen to him every day – and then bumps into a chair which falls over.

Left alone with Lopakhin, Dooniasha reveals that Yepihodov has recently proposed to her. Dooniasha, however, does not appear to be very interested.

Coaches are heard outside, and Lopakhin and Dooniasha go out of the room, leaving the stage empty. Soon Feers, the aged servant, crosses the stage, muttering to himself. Briefly, the stage is empty again, while the noises outside get louder. Then the room is suddenly filled with people: Liubov enters, followed by Ania, her daughter, Charlotta, the governess, Varia, who is Liubov's adopted daughter, Gayev, Liubov's brother, Simeonov-Pishchik, a landowner, Lopakhin, and Dooniasha.

Delighted to be back in her old nursery, Liubov kisses her brother, Varia, and Dooniasha. Charlotta astonishes Pishchik by claiming that her dog eats nuts. Then everybody except Ania and Dooniasha leave the room.

Although Ania complains of feeling cold and exhausted, Dooniasha cannot wait to blurt out the news of Yepihodov's proposal. Ania, however, takes no interest: she has heard this many times before. Ania is delighted to be back in her own room and looks forward to going out into the orchard. Dooniasha tells her that Trofimov has arrived but is sleeping in the bath-house.

Varia enters and tells Dooniasha to make some coffee for Liubov. Varia and Ania embrace, and Ania goes on to speak of the difficulties during her journey to Paris. She has found Charlotta a tiresome companion, and her mother's way of life in Paris has made her feel sad and depressed. Having had to sell her villa in Mentone, Liubov has had no money left, yet she has continued to live extravagantly. Varia reveals to Ania that they have been unable to pay the interest due on their debts. As a result, the estate will be up for sale in August.

Lopakhin puts his head through the door and bleats like a sheep, provoking an angry outburst from Varia. She tells her sister that although everybody is talking of her wedding and even congratulating her, Lopakhin has not yet proposed to her, and Varia no longer thinks that he ever will. Varia would like to marry Ania off to some rich man. Then she herself would go to a hermitage and, subsequently, on a pilgrimage to holy places.

As Dooniasha prepares the coffee, Yasha, Liubov's servant, asks if he can go through the room. Dooniasha finds that Yasha has changed while abroad. Calling Dooniasha 'a little peach', Yasha suddenly puts his arms around her, making Dooniasha cry out and drop a saucer.

Ania tells Varia that they ought to warn Liubov that Trofimov has arrived. Trofimov used to be the tutor of Liubov's son, Grisha, who was drowned at the age of seven, soon after the death of Liubov's husband. In her sorrow, Liubov went abroad. Now Ania is worried that the sight of Trofimov will evoke unhappy memories and make Liubov depressed.

Feers comes in and prepares to serve coffee. He is so delighted that his mistress is home that he weeps with joy.

Liubov, Lopakhin, Gayev, and Pishchik enter. Ania retires to bed, and Varia tells Lopakhin and Pishchik that it is time to break up the party. Liubov assures Varia that they will leave as soon as they have had some coffee.

Liubov still cannot believe that she is back home. Speaking of her love of her country, she claims that she was crying so much while travelling through it that she could not see it properly. Turning to Feers, she tells him how glad she is to have found him still alive. But Feers cannot hear very well, and his reply makes no sense.

Lopakhin is annoyed that he is having to go to Kharkov: he would have preferred to stay and talk to Liubov. He is anxious that Liubov should retain her faith in him, for although his father has been a serf on the estate, Liubov, Lopakhin says, has done so much for him that he loves her as if she were his own sister.

Excited and agitated, Liubov jumps up and walks about, kissing a bookcase and speaking appreciatively of a small table. Gayev reminds her that their old nanny has died while Liubov has been abroad.

Lopakhin reveals that he has a plan which will enable the family to keep the estate. Fortunately, the estate is close to the town and the railway, and Lopakhin suggests that the land along the river be divided into plots and leased to people from the town, who would build summer cottages on their plots. The old buildings would have to be demolished and the orchard cut down, but the income would solve the family's financial problems.

Gayev and Liubov are unable to understand. Liubov points out that their orchard is outstanding in the whole country, and Gayev reminds Lopakhin that it is mentioned in the Encyclopaedia. Lopakhin retorts that they must make a decision and that there is no solution other than the one he has just suggested. Feers recalls how the cherries from the orchard used to be dried, preserved, marinaded, and made into jam. The dried cherries provided a good income; unfortunately, however, the recipe for drying them has been lost.

Pishchik asks Liubov if she has eaten frogs in Paris, and she astonishes him by replying that she has eaten crocodiles. Lopakhin expands on his plans for the estate, suggesting that the new summer residents may start cultivating their plots of land, 'and then your cherry orchard would be gay with life and wealth and luxury'.

Varia hands Liubov two telegrams. Noticing that they have come from Paris, Liubov tears them up without reading them.

Gayev points out that the old bookcase, from which Varia has taken the telegrams, is a hundred years old. He then addresses the bookcase, claiming that for a hundred years, it has 'never failed to fill us with an urge to useful work', and that it has 'fostered in us the ideal of public good and social consciousness'. When Liubov comments that Gayev is just the same as he always has been, he gets embarrassed and resorts to his imaginary game of billiards.

Yasha brings Liubov's medicines. Claiming that medicines do neither good nor harm, Pishchik swallows the contents of Liubov's box of pills. The others are astonished.

Charlotta Ivanovna enters, wearing a white dress. Lopakhin tries to kiss her hand, but Charlotta refuses. She is equally unwilling to perform tricks for them.

Lopakhin says goodbye. As he turns to Liubov, reminding her to consider his plan seriously, Varia becomes impatient and tells him to leave. Gayev complains about Lopakhin being a boor but then apologises: Varia, he knows, is going to marry Lopakhin.

Pishchik drops off to sleep but wakes up at once to ask Liubov to lend him some money so that he can pay the interest on his mortgage. On learning that Liubov has not got any money, Pishchik is not unduly worried. He is convinced that the money he needs will turn up.

Varia opens a window towards the orchard, and Gayev and Liubov join her, admiring the sight of the white trees in the morning sun. Liubov speaks of her happy childhood. She is envious of the orchard's capacity for renewal every spring; by contrast, she can never feel free from the burden of her past life. Liubov suddenly imagines that she can see her mother walking through the orchard; but the figure turns out to be a small white cherry tree, bending over slightly.

Trofimov enters. Greeting Liubov, he explains that he has been too impatient to wait until the morning before seeing her. When Liubov recognises Trofimov, she embraces him and weeps. But she soon regains her composure. She finds that Trofimov has changed a lot: he used to be good-looking, but now his hair is thin and he wears spectacles. Trofimov confirms that he is still a student; indeed, he tells Liubov, he expects to remain a student until the end of his life.

Liubov kisses her brother and Varia good night. Pishchik follows her, insisting on borrowing the two hundred and forty roubles he so badly needs.

Gayev, Varia, and Yasha remain in the nursery. Gayev comments on Liubov's habit of throwing money away. Besides, he is irritated with Yasha. Varia finally succeeds in making Yasha leave by telling him that his mother has been waiting for him in the servants' hall since the previous day.

Gayev and Varia discuss the possibilities of saving the estate. Gayev presents a range of solutions: they may inherit some money, or they may be able to marry Ania off to some wealthy man, or their rich aunt in Yaroslavl might help them. Weeping, Varia prefers to put her trust in God. Gayev insists that their aunt would be a better alternative. The only difficulty is that she has never approved of Liubov's marriage, far less of her moral standards. As Gayev criticises Liubov's morality, Ania eavesdrops. After a warning from Varia, Gayev abruptly changes the subject.

Ania enters. Gayev kisses her, but Ania tells her uncle that he ought to keep quiet rather than talk. Gayev admits that Ania is right, and he agrees that his address to the bookcase was foolish. Varia, too, asks Gayev to keep quiet, and he agrees – only to go on to tell his nieces about his recent visit to the District Court and his hopes that they may be able to get a loan on promissory notes. Liubov, Gayev says, is going to try to borrow money from Lopakhin; and Ania is to be sent to Yaroslavl, to see her rich aunt. Gayev claims to be convinced that this three-pronged approach will succeed. Considerably calmer and happier, Ania embraces her uncle.

Feers enters. Is not Gayev ashamed of himself, he asks; when is he going to bed? Calming Feers down, Gayev tells Varia and Ania that it is time to go to bed. Before leaving, Gayev embarks on another speech, but

Ania and Varia manage to cut him off in mid-sentence. After another stern reminder from Feers, Gayev finally retires to bed.

Ania tells Varia that she is feeling more relieved now, and grateful to their uncle. Varia starts describing something that has happened while Ania has been away, but when she realises that Ania has fallen asleep, she helps her to get into bed. As they leave, the sound of a shepherd's pipe can be heard from outside. Trofimov enters. Only when Varia and Ania have disappeared into Ania's room does he speak: 'Ania . . . ,' he says, 'my one bright star! My spring flower!'

NOTES AND GLOSSARY:

kvass:	Russian rye-beer
Lent:	a forty-day period in the Christian year, from Ash Wednesday to Easter Eve. To commemorate Christ's fasting in the wilderness, this period is traditionally devoted to fasting and penitence
Mentone:	a town on the French Riviera
patchouli:	an East Indian plant with a strong smell
Kharkov:	a town in the Ukraine, in Russia
Encyclopaedia:	a work giving information on all branches of knowledge or on one subject. The information is usually arranged alphabetically
Holy Week:	the week before Easter Sunday
Au revoir:	(*French*) goodbye
mortgage:	a loan with property as security
Yaroslavl:	a town situated on the Volga
promissory notes:	signed documents containing a written promise to pay the stated sum to a specified person or to the bearer at a specified date or on demand

Act 2

Act 2 is set in the open country. By the roadside are an old shrine, a well, a seat, and some large stones, which apparently used to be gravestones. A road leads to Gayev's estate, and there is a row of poplars where the cherry orchard begins. A line of telegraph poles is visible, as are the outlines of a large town on the horizon. The sun is about to set.

Charlotta, Yasha, and Dooniasha are sitting on the seat, and nearby stands Yepihodov, playing the guitar. Charlotta, who is holding a shotgun, begins to speak. Her parents, she explains, used to perform at fairs and taught her a variety of tricks. After their death, she was brought up by a German lady, and eventually she became a governess. But she is troubled by the uncertainty surrounding her origin and identity, and also by the fact that she has no one to speak to.

Yepihodov plays and sings, but when he claims that his guitar is a mandoline, Dooniasha, who is busy powdering her face, objects sharply. Yepihodov retorts that to a man who is crazy with love, the guitar is indeed a mandoline, and when he goes on singing, Yasha joins in. Charlotta finds their singing dreadful. Ignoring Yepihodov, Dooniasha turns to Yasha, flattering him by taking an interest in his travels abroad. Yawning, Yasha lights a cigar.

Yepihodov takes up the theme of life abroad and claims to be a cultured person himself, having read 'all sorts of extraordinary books'. Yet, he says awkwardly, he does not really know what he wants, whether he wants to live or to shoot himself. Just in case, he always carries a revolver.

Making a sarcastic comment to Yepihodov, Charlotta leaves. But Yepihodov goes on to explain that fate is merciless to him, striking him with one misfortune after the other. Turning to Dooniasha, he asks to speak to her alone, but as if to confirm his words about his misfortunes, Dooniasha sends him away to get her cape from the house. Commenting, melodramatically, that now he knows what to do with his revolver, Yepihodov walks away, leaving Dooniasha and Yasha alone.

Now it is Dooniasha's turn to speak of herself. Explaining that she has been a servant on the estate since she was a little girl, she claims to have become as sensitive and delicate as any member of the family. Yasha kisses her, commenting at the same time that a girl should behave herself: girls who are too free with men arouse his dislike. Indeed, he is of the opinion that 'if a girl loves somebody, it means she's immoral.'

People are heard approaching. Dooniasha puts her arm around Yasha, but he tells her to go away; the last thing he wants is to make his mistress suspect that he has been alone with Dooniasha.

Complaining about the smell of Yasha's cigar, Dooniasha leaves, and Yasha remains alone by the shrine. Liubov, Gayev, and Lopakhin enter. Lopakhin is insisting that Liubov and Gayev make up their minds about the future of the estate. But Liubov studiously ignores Lopakhin's plea; instead, she comments on the abominable smell of Yasha's cigar, thus unwittingly echoing Dooniasha's complaint. Gayev also ignores Lopakhin and turns to praising the advantages of railway travel.

Liubov complains that although she has had a lot of money, she now has virtually nothing left. The members of the family are reduced to living off milk soups, and the servants get nothing but dried peas. In a paradoxical illustration of her point, Liubov then drops her purse, and gold coins are scattered on the ground. As Yasha starts picking them up, Liubov speaks of the restaurant where they have just been. Liubov is extremely critical of it, and the behaviour of her brother has only made matters worse. Gayev appears to take Liubov's criticism very calmly, but his irritation surfaces when he turns to Yasha and forces him to leave.

Refusing to let slip the subject of the estate, Lopakhin reveals that a wealthy man wants to buy it at the auction. Gayev tells Lopakhin that their aunt in Yaroslavl has promised them money, but when Lopakhin wants to know the exact sum, Liubov has to admit that it will not be a large one.

Lopakhin is finding it increasingly difficult to control his temper. Calling Liubov and Gayev 'feckless, unbusiness-like, [and] queer', he claims that he cannot understand their attitude. Liubov retorts that villas and summer visitors are 'vulgar', and her brother agrees. Lopakhin is exasperated and threatens to leave. But Liubov implores him to stay, arguing, paradoxically, that 'somehow it's more cheerful with you here.'

Liubov admits that she keeps feeling as if the house were about to fall down on them. Gayev, on his part, hides his thoughts beneath his customary billiard terms. Implying that the disaster threatening the estate is due to her own way of life, Liubov starts speaking of her past 'sins'. The man she married was a drunkard, who was always in debt. After the death of her husband, she had an affair with another man. When her son was drowned, she saw this as a punishment. She fled abroad, intending never to return. But her lover followed her, and when he fell ill, Liubov bought a villa on the French Riviera where she nursed him for three years. Eventually the villa had to be sold to pay her debts, and Liubov went to Paris, where her lover took her money and then went to live with another woman. Liubov tried to commit suicide. Then she decided to return to Russia. She concludes her story by taking out a telegram, which she has just received from Paris: her lover is asking her to forgive him and begging her to return.

Music is heard, and on learning that it is a well-known Jewish band playing, Liubov suggests that the musicians be invited to the house so that they can have a dance. Unlike Liubov and Gayev, Lopakhin cannot hear the music. Instead, he speaks of a play which he has seen recently. Liubov tells Lopakhin that instead of going to the theatre he should take a look at himself: is not his life a drab one, and is he not speaking a lot of nonsense? Lopakhin admits that she is right. Liubov tells Lopakhin that he ought to get married, and he agrees, but without enthusiasm. Pointing out that Varia would make a good wife, Liubov starts listing her excellent qualities. Lopakhin, however, does not seem very impressed.

Gayev reveals that he has been offered a post at the bank. But the news does not have the impact that Gayev has clearly expected; on the contrary, his sister bluntly tells him that he had better stay where he is.

Feers arrives with an overcoat which he tells Gayev to put on against the evening chill. He proceeds to rebuke Gayev for having left in the morning without telling him. Liubov comments that Feers has aged, but he does not hear what she is saying. When her comment is repeated, he begins to speak of his long life, and, especially, of the abolition of serfdom. Feers, who was already a chief valet when serfdom was abolished, preferred to stay with his master and mistress rather than take his freedom. Feers praises the past, only to provoke a sarcastic comment from Lopakhin, who agrees that it was 'a good life all right! At least, people got flogged!' Again, Feers fails to hear what is being said and continues his own line of thought: what made the past so good, he explains, was that both the gentry and the peasants knew where they belonged. Now, he is implying, society is disintegrating.

Gayev speaks of going to town the following day: he is hoping that one of his contacts will help them to get a loan. But Lopakhin is convinced that nothing will come of Gayev's efforts, and Liubov agrees with him.

Trofimov, Ania, and Varia appear. Liubov embraces Ania and Varia and asks them to sit down beside her. Lopakhin makes an ironic comment about the 'eternal student', who is always with the young ladies. When Trofimov wants to know why Lopakhin keeps pestering him, Lopakhin turns the attention on to himself, asking what Trofimov thinks of him. Trofimov's reply is blunt: Lopakhin, who he believes will soon be a millionaire, is no more than a necessary evil, to be equalled with a wild beast.

Varia and Liubov attempt to change the topic, and they return to discussing pride, the subject of the previous day. Trofimov wonders why anybody should be proud when man, in most cases, is in fact 'coarse, stupid, and profoundly unhappy'. He argues for an end to all self-admiration; instead everybody should work, and work hard. Trofimov believes that humanity is advancing and making progress all the time, but only dedicated work will bring perfection within reach. He is full of contempt for the members of the intelligentsia who spend their time discussing and philosophising, but achieve nothing – and this while servants and peasants are having to lead miserable lives in poverty and squalor. Lopakhin retorts that he himself works very hard. He is also well aware of what people around him are like, and he does not share Trofimov's optimism: if anything, Lopakhin has been saddened by the dearth of honest and decent people. In a country of such vast proportions as their own, Lopakhin argues, they ought to be giants.

Liubov objects to Lopakhin's reference to giants: they belong in fairy-tales, she says, but otherwise they are just frightening.

Yepihodov, playing his guitar, crosses the stage in the background. Pointing out that the sun has set, Gayev embarks on a passionate address to nature. Varia, Ania, and Trofimov stop him, and silence ensues. Suddenly, as if out of the sky, comes a strange sound, as of a string snapping.

Everybody comes up with a different explanation of the sound. Lopakhin thinks that a lift cable may have broken in a distant mine, while Gayev believes that it may have been a heron, and Trofimov suggests an owl. Liubov shudders, having found the sound unpleasant, and Feers remembers that similar strange sounds were heard before 'the misfortune', by which he means the abolition of serfdom.

A tramp appears. He asks the way to the railway station and then begs some money from Varia. She is frightened, but Liubov takes out her purse and hands the tramp a gold coin. Varia is unable to understand how Liubov can give the tramp so much money when they have no food in the house. Liubov, however, is resigned to the fact that she is incapable of handling money. Instead, she turns to Lopakhin, asking him to lend her some. She also tells Varia that her marriage to Lopakhin has been virtually arranged. Varia protests against Liubov's frivolous treatment of the subject; while Lopakhin quotes from Shakespeare's *Hamlet*, choosing his speeches so as to imply that Varia is more interested in becoming a nun than in marrying him.

Trofimov and Ania are left alone. Ania is particularly pleased that the tramp has frightened Varia away. Trofimov confirms that Varia nearly always follows them, worried as she is that Trofimov and Ania will fall in love. But Varia, Trofimov asserts, is narrow-minded: she cannot understand that he and Ania are above falling in love. All that matters to Trofimov is the march forward. Ania is impressed by the way in which Trofimov speaks. At the same time, she is puzzled by his effect on her: she used to think that their cherry orchard was the best place in the world, but now she no longer loves it as she used to. Trofimov explains that the whole of Russia is their orchard. Ania should remember, he says, that all her forefathers owned serfs: 'Don't you see human beings gazing at you from every cherry tree in your orchard, from every leaf and every tree-trunk, don't you hear voices?'. As a result, Trofimov claims, Ania and all the members of her family have become perverted. They do not realise that they are living in perpetual debt, 'at the expense of people you don't admit further than the kitchen'. According to Trofimov, they shall have to atone for the past, and this is possible only by suffering. Ania promises him that she will leave the family house, and Trofimov approves, saying that she will be free as the wind if she does. Again, he insists that Ania must believe him: he has suffered so much, having spent many years as a poor student, and yet great hopes and visions continue to fill his soul. He is convinced that happiness is coming.

Ania notices that the moon is rising. Yepihodov can be heard playing his guitar, and somewhere by the poplars Varia is looking for Ania and calling for her.

Trofimov again confirms that happiness is indeed coming; even if they will not be seeing it themselves, others will.

Varia calls. Ania suggests that they go down to the river, and she and Trofimov go out together. Again, Varia is heard calling for her sister.

NOTES AND GLOSSARY:

salto-mortale: (*Italian*) literally 'deadly leap'; a somersault beginning with a standing jump

Buckle: Henry Thomas Buckle (1821–62), English historian

the decadents: 'The name "decadent" was sometimes given to the symbolist movement in literature and art of the end of the nineteenth century.' (Hingley, *The Oxford Chekhov*, III, 335)

when Freedom was granted to the people: Feers is speaking of the emancipation of the serfs in 1861

Yet all the time . . . immorality everywhere: the censor objected to this sentence, and Chekhov had to replace it with one couched in more moderate terms

Oh, my brother, my suffering brother! . . . : from a poem by Nadson (1862–87)

Come to mother Volga . . . : from a poem by Nekrasov (1821–78)

Go to a nunnery, Ohmelia!: Lopakhin is quoting from Shakespeare's *Hamlet* (III.i.121): 'Get thee to a nunnery.' Lopakhin's form of the name Ophelia is a pun; in Hingley's words, 'it is tempting to translate: "Ophelia – hop along and get thee to a nunnery"' (Hingley, *The Oxford Chekhov*, III, 335)

Ohmelia, oh nymph, remember me in thy orisons!: 'Nymph, in thy orisons/Be all my sins remembered' (*Hamlet*, III.i.88). *Orisons* means 'prayers'. Lopakhin continues to pun on the name Ophelia, and here Hingley suggests the following translation: 'Nymph, in thy orisons be all my sins – and double gins – remembered' (Hingley, *The Oxford Chekhov*, III, 335)

They owned . . . further than the kitchen: this sentence, too, was criticised by the censor, and Chekhov had to supply an alternative version

Act 3

Act 3 is set in the drawing-room of Liubov Andryeevna's house. The ballroom can be seen through an archway at the back. It is evening, and a band is heard playing. A party is dancing in the ballroom. Soon they all come into the drawing-room, Pishchik dancing with Charlotta, Trofimov with Liubov, Ania with the post-office clerk, and Varia with the station-master. Dooniasha is in the last couple.

The dance ends. Feers crosses the room, and Pishchik and Trofimov come back into the drawing-room. Pishchik complains that he is suffering from high blood-pressure but then goes on to assert that he is as strong as a horse. His main concern, however, is money, of which he is always short. Pishchik falls asleep, snores, and then wakes up again, to tell Trofimov that he cannot think of anything but money.

Someone can be heard playing billiards in the room next door. When Varia appears in the ballroom, Trofimov teases her, calling her 'Madame Lopakhin'. Varia retaliates by calling Trofimov the 'moth-eaten gent'. Varia is worried about the fact that they have hired a band for which they cannot pay.

Trofimov suggests to Pishchik that if he had made better use of the energy he has wasted during a lifetime of looking for money to pay the interest on his debts, he might have been able to achieve great things. Pishchik claims that Nietzsche says that it is justifiable to forge bank-notes. Pressed by Trofimov, he has to admit that he has not read Nietzsche: he has the information from his daughter. Just now, Pishchik says, he would very much like to forge some bank-notes: in two days' time, he will have to pay three hundred and ten roubles, and so far, he has been able to borrow less than half that sum. Pishchik starts feeling in his pockets for the money, but cannot find it. In mounting desperation he searches all his pockets, and eventually finds the money.

Liubov and Charlotta enter. Liubov is singing a popular dance tune. She is worried about her brother, who has not yet returned from town. Trofimov suggests that the auction may never have taken place. Liubov says that the band arrived at the wrong time and the party started at the wrong time – but then she brushes it all aside with a 'never mind' and continues to sing.

Charlotta performs some card tricks, first with Pishchik and then with Trofimov. She then turns to ventriloquism. Pishchik declares that he is quite in love with her, but Charlotta does not take him very seriously. She then performs another trick: taking a rug from a chair, she holds it up, as if offering it for sale, but when she suddenly lifts it up, Ania is found to be standing behind it. Charlotta repeats the trick, and this time Varia is standing behind the rug. Charlotta's audience is delighted, and when she leaves the room, Pishchik follows her.

Liubov returns to her worries: Gayev still has not come back. She is annoyed that he is keeping them in ignorance: by now either the estate must have been sold, or the auction never took place. Varia is convinced that Gayev has bought the estate, for her grandmother has given him permission to buy the estate in her name and transfer the mortgage to her. Liubov puts Varia right: her grandmother has only sent fifteen thousand roubles, which is not even enough to pay the interest. On this day, Liubov says, her fate is being decided.

Again, Trofimov teases Varia by calling her 'Madame Lopakhin'. Varia gets angry, pointing out that Trofimov has been thrown out of the university twice. But Liubov cannot understand why Varia should be so annoyed: Lopakhin, she points out, is a nice and interesting person. Varia agrees, and admits that she likes Lopakhin. But although everybody has been talking of the two of them for years, Lopakhin has not yet proposed to her. Varia believes that his business is more important to him than she can ever be. She herself would prefer to become a nun. What she cannot bear, she tells Liubov, is to be without work: she must have work to do all the time.

Yasha comes in to report that Yepihodov has broken a billiard cue. Varia is upset to learn that Yepihodov is being allowed to play billiards. She follows Yasha out of the room.

Alone with Trofimov, Liubov tells him not to tease Varia so much. Trofimov complains that Varia has not left him and Ania alone all summer; she has not realised that he and Ania are above falling in love. Liubov comments, with bitterness, that in that case she herself is presumably below love. Again, she speaks of Gayev and her anxiety about the fate of the estate. She is feeling so upset that she could cry out loud or do something silly, and she asks Trofimov to help her by speaking to her. Trofimov suggests to her that it makes no difference whether the estate is sold on this particular day or not: the old way of life is finished, and now Liubov must face up to the truth. Liubov wants to know what truth Trofimov is referring to. He seems to have no difficulties solving his problems, but Liubov wonders if this is not merely due to the fact that he is young and inexperienced: Trofimov, she says, has not yet suffered as a result of his problems. She asks him to be generous to people like herself. She on her part cannot imagine life without the cherry orchard; indeed, if the orchard has to be sold, she would prefer to be sold with it. Embracing Trofimov and kissing him on his forehead, Liubov reminds him that her son was drowned on the estate. Trofimov says that he sympathises with her, but his words leave her dissatisfied. As she takes out her handkerchief, a telegram falls on the floor. Liubov assures Trofimov that she loves him as if he were her own child, and that she would be happy to let Ania marry him, but first he must study and finish his course. And, she says, Trofimov ought to do something to make his beard grow.

Trofimov picks up the telegram, and Liubov explains that it has come from Paris: she is getting one every day. Her lover is ill again and wants her to come back. Liubov admits that she will probably obey his call, for she loves him and cannot be without him.

Trofimov tells Liubov that her lover has been robbing her of her money, but Liubov does not want to listen to him. When he goes on to criticise her lover, Liubov complains that Trofimov, despite his age, is still like a schoolboy. He ought to be able to understand people who are in love; indeed, he ought to be able to fall in love himself. Horrifying Trofimov, Liubov tells him that he is nothing but a crank and a freak, and that at his age, he ought to have a mistress. Trofimov walks out, only to return to tell Liubov that everything is finished between them. Liubov calls after him that she has merely been joking, but Trofimov refuses to listen. Instead there comes from the hall the sound of someone running upstairs and then falling down with a crash. Ania and Varia are heard to cry out and then laugh, and Ania comes running in to report that Trofimov has fallen down the stairs.

Standing in the middle of the ballroom, the station-master begins to recite a poem called 'The Sinner'. But the band soon strikes up a waltz, and everybody dances. Trofimov returns from the hall, and Liubov asks his forgiveness. They dance.

Feers comes in and stands his walking stick by the door. He is accompanied by Yasha. Feers is not feeling very well. He speaks of the balls they used to have in the past, attended by generals, barons, and admirals; now, by contrast, they are having to make do with people like the post-office clerk and the station-master. Yasha, however, is not interested in Feers's patter. Feers wearies him, and he wishes that the old servant would go away and die soon.

Having danced with Trofimov, Liubov sits down in the drawing-room. Ania comes in to report that a man in the kitchen has said that the cherry orchard has been sold. Then Ania dances with Trofimov.

Yasha confirms that a stranger has been in the kitchen. Now Feers, too, is worried about Gayev, especially since he is only wearing his light overcoat, and may catch a cold.

Liubov asks Yasha to find out who has bought the estate. Laughing, Yasha tells her that the stranger has been gone a long time. Annoyed by Yasha's laughing, Liubov wants to know what he is so happy about, and Yasha replies that he finds Yepihodov such a comic person.

Turning to Feers, Liubov asks him where he will go if the estate is sold. Feers answers that he will go wherever she orders him. Liubov wonders if he is ill and suggests he go to bed. Feers points out that if he were to retire to bed there would be nobody to wait on the guests and keep things going.

Yasha implores Liubov to take him with her if she returns to Paris. He is finding his fellow servants too uneducated and immoral for his taste.

Pishchik comes in to ask Liubov for a dance. As they walk into the ballroom, he tries to borrow money from her.

Charlotta, wearing check trousers and a grey top hat, can be seen jumping in the air and throwing her arms about in the ballroom.

Dooniasha powders her face. As there are so few ladies, Liubov has ordered her to dance, but dancing is making her dizzy. She tells Feers that the post-office clerk has just likened her to a flower. Dooniasha is very much taken in by the compliment, but neither Feers, nor Yasha, who happens to overhear her, are very impressed.

Yepihodov comes in, complaining that Dooniasha does not seem to want to look at him any more. He embarks on a clumsy speech, but Dooniasha is impatient and asks to be left alone.

Varia enters from the ballroom. She is annoyed to find Yepihodov in the drawing-room. Asking Dooniasha to leave, she starts telling Yepihodov off: first he plays billiards and breaks a cue, and then he walks round the drawing-room as if he were a visitor to the house. When Yepihodov defends his actions, Varia is infuriated and orders him out of the house. Following him to the door, she tells him that she never wants to see him again. Varia arms herself with the stick that Feers has left by the door, and when she believes that Yepihodov is about to re-enter the drawing-room, she swings the stick – only to discover that the person she is about to hit is Lopakhin.

Varia is angry that she should have appeared to threaten Lopakhin, and she asks him to confirm that she has not hurt him. Joking, Lopakhin tells her that he has got a big bump coming up.

The people in the ballroom have realised that Lopakhin has arrived, and Pishchik and Liubov join him. Liubov asks for her brother, and Lopakhin informs her that he and Gayev have returned from town together. When Liubov asks about the auction, Lopakhin is embarrassed, but he tells her that the auction was over by four o'clock. He and Gayev have missed the train.

Gayev enters, carrying some parcels and wiping away his tears. Liubov wants to know what has happened, but Gayev merely waves his hand at her. He tells Feers to take the parcels, which contain anchovies and Kerch herrings. Gayev complains that he has had nothing to eat all day.

The sound of people playing billiards next door brings about a change in Gayev's expression, and he stops crying. Claiming that he is extremely tired, he tells Feers to come and then leaves the room.

Pishchik and Liubov again turn to Lopakhin, asking him to reveal what has happened at the auction. Lopakhin confirms that the orchard has been sold. Liubov asks who bought it, and Lopakhin replies, 'I did.'

There is a pause. Liubov has to support herself against a table and a chair so as not to collapse. Varia takes the keys of the house from her belt and throws them on the floor. Then she walks out.

Lopakhin gives an account of what has happened at the auction. He can hardly believe that he, who used to be beaten frequently, who can barely read, and who used to run about with bare feet in the middle of winter, now owns 'the most beautiful place on God's earth'. Lopakhin has succeeded in buying the estate where his father and grandfather were serfs. Now, Lopakhin says, the trees in the orchard will come down, villas will be built, and their children and grandchildren will see a new world grow up where the orchard has stood.

The band plays. Liubov is sitting in a chair, crying bitterly. Lopakhin asks why she did not listen to his advice. Now it is too late to change things. When he continues, he is speaking '*with great emotion*': 'Oh, if only we could be done with all this', Lopakhin says, 'if only we could alter this distorted unhappy life somehow!'

Pishchik tells Lopakhin to leave Liubov alone. As they walk towards the ballroom, Lopakhin orders the band to play up: now everything must be as he wishes it. He makes an ironic reference to himself as the new landowner – and then accidentally hits a small table, nearly making some candlesticks fall over. But it does not matter, Lopakhin says; he can pay for everything.

Both the ballroom and the drawing-room are empty except for Liubov, who is still crying in her chair. The band can be heard playing.

Ania and Trofimov enter. Ania kneels beside her mother, telling her not to cry. It is true that the orchard has been sold, she says, but Liubov still has her life ahead of her. They will go away, and they will plant a new orchard, even more splendid than the old one. When her mother sees this orchard, Ania asserts, she will understand everything and her heart will be filled with happiness.

NOTES AND GLOSSARY:

the Grand-Rond: a kind of dance

Promenade à une paire!: (*French*) Walk in pairs!

Grand rond balancez!: (*French*) *balancez* here means 'take position facing your partner'

Les cavaliers ... vos dames!: (*French*) The gentlemen kneel; thank your ladies!

the very same horse that Caligula sat in the Senate: Caligula (AD 12–41) was a Roman Emperor, known for his cruelty and recklessness. According to one of the many anecdotes told about Caligula, he had plans to appoint his favourite racehorse to the office of consul. The consul was the chairman of the Roman senate

Nietzsche: Friedrich Nietzsche (1844–1900), German philosopher

Ein, zwei, drei!: (*German*) One, two, three!

Guter Mensch aber schlechter Musikant: (*German*) A good man but a bad musician. Charlotta is saying that although Pishchik is a pleasant man, he is not very sensitive

power of attorney: authority for one person to act for another

weigh ton: read 'weight on'

| 'The Sinner': | a poem by Alexyei Tolstoy (1817–75). Hingley translates the title as 'The Sinful Woman', thus indicating a reference to Liubov |
| **Kerch herrings:** | herring from the Crimean seaport of Kerch |

Act 4

Like the first act of *The Cherry Orchard*, the last act is set in the nursery on the estate. But now the room is virtually empty. The curtains and the pictures have been removed, furniture has been piled up in a corner, and at the back of the room luggage has been lined up.

Lopakhin stands waiting, and Yasha is holding a tray full of glasses of champagne. In the hall, Yepihodov is securing a big box with string. Outside, Gayev can be heard saying goodbye to the peasants.

Liubov and Gayev enter. Gayev tells his sister that she should not have given the peasants her purse, but Liubov replies that she could not help herself. As they leave the room, Lopakhin calls after them, offering them some champagne, but they both decline the offer. Lopakhin then suggests that Yasha has some champagne, and the servant drinks – only to complain of the quality of Lopakhin's champagne. Lopakhin replies that he has paid eight roubles a bottle.

Lopakhin is finding the house cold, and Yasha explains that the stoves have not been lit. Although it is October, it is sunny and calm, which to Lopakhin means 'good building weather'. Looking at his watch, Lopakhin finds that they have forty-six minutes to spare before the train is due to leave.

Trofimov enters. He is wearing an overcoat, and is looking for his goloshes. He announces that the horses are waiting. Lopakhin explains that he shall be leaving on the same train as the family, to spend the winter in Kharkov. Remaining on the estate, without any work to do, is torture to Lopakhin: without any work to do, his hands begin to feel limp and strange, as if they did not belong to him.

Lopakhin offers Trofimov a drink, but Trofimov declines. He confirms that he will be going to Moscow. When Lopakhin pesters Trofimov about his never-ending studies, Trofimov changes the subject. 'By way of a farewell', he wants to give Lopakhin some advice. He tells Lopakhin to stop throwing his arms about, and compares his sweeping gestures to his plans for building villas and turning summer residents into smallholders. Yet he claims to like Lopakhin, and he compares his fingers to those of an artist, saying that Lopakhin has 'a fine, sensitive soul'. Lopakhin offers Trofimov some money for his journey, but the student turns down the offer. He is still looking for his goloshes when Varia throws in a pair of goloshes from the room next door, but Trofimov protests that they are not his.

Lopakhin explains that he has just made forty thousand roubles from the poppies he has grown, and for this reason he can offer Trofimov some money. Trofimov maintains that he would never borrow any sum of money from Lopakhin: he regards himself as a free man, and money, so important to rich and poor alike, is to him 'just so much fluff blowing about in the air'. Humanity, Trofimov asserts, is advancing towards the highest truth with himself in the forefront, and he can do without people like Lopakhin. When Lopakhin wants to know whether Trofimov will reach this great goal himself, he replies 'yes'; but after a pause, he adds: 'I'll get there myself, or show others the way to get there.'

The sound of an axe striking a tree is heard in the distance. 'We show off in front of one another', Lopakhin says to Trofimov, 'and in the meantime life is slipping by.' Lopakhin claims that he feels most happy when working hard, but, he implies, few people in Russia do anything useful. As an example, he mentions Gayev, who has taken up his post at the bank: Lopakhin believes that Gayev is so lazy that he will not stay at the bank for very long.

Ania appears in the doorway: her mother is asking Lopakhin not to start cutting down the orchard until she has left. Trofimov comes out in support of Liubov and Ania, and asks if Lopakhin has not got any tact. Reluctantly, Lopakhin agrees to their request.

Ania asks Yasha whether Feers has been taken to hospital, and Yasha believes that he has. When Ania turns to Yepihodov, telling him to find out what has happened to Feers, Yasha is annoyed that she has not believed what he has said. Yepihodov thinks that it is time that Feers joined his ancestors.

Varia, too, wants to know if Feers has been taken to hospital; if he has, she cannot understand why the letter to the doctor has been left behind. Speaking from the room next door, Varia announces that Yasha's mother has arrived and wants to say goodbye to him. But Yasha merely waves his hand, claiming that he is losing his patience with his mother.

Dooniasha has been attending to the luggage, but when Yasha is alone, she comes up to him. Crying, she puts her arms around his neck, complaining that he is leaving her behind. Paying no attention to Dooniasha's sorrow, Yasha drinks more champagne and waxes enthusiastic about France. He tells Dooniasha to behave like a respectable girl; then there will be no need to cry. Dooniasha looks into a mirror and powders her nose. She asks Yasha to write to her from Paris.

Someone can be heard coming, and Yasha pretends to be busy with a suitcase. Liubov, Gayev, Ania, and Charlotta enter. Gayev points out that there is not much time left. Looking at Yasha, he wonders who is smelling of herring.

Liubov begins to say goodbye to the old house. Winter will pass, she says, and when spring comes the house will be pulled down. Kissing Ania and commenting on her radiant eyes, Liubov asks if she is happy, and Ania confirms that she is: 'Our new life is just beginning', she says. Gayev agrees that everything is much better now: before the auction, everybody was worried and upset, but now they have calmed down and even feel quite cheerful. He has found employment, and his sister, too, is looking better. Liubov confirms that her nerves have improved, and that she is sleeping better at night. Turning to Ania, Liubov says that they will soon be seeing each other again. She herself will be going to Paris, where she will be living off the money that Ania's grandmother has sent towards buying the estate; and this money, Liubov knows, will not last very long. Ania asks her mother to come back soon. In the meantime, she will study and pass her school examinations, and when Liubov returns they will read all kinds of books together, 'and a new, wonderful world will open up before us'.

Lopakhin enters. Charlotta sings quietly to herself. Picking up a bundle that looks like a baby in swaddling clothes, Charlotta pretends to say goodbye to it, and as the sound of a baby crying is heard, she continues to speak to the bundle in her arms. But soon she throws the bundle down, asking if she will be found another job, for she cannot manage without one. Lopakhin assures her that they will find her a job.

Pishchik appears, much out of breath. Gayev, who is sure that Pishchik has come to borrow money, apologises and leaves the room. But Pishchik unexpectedly hands some money to Lopakhin, explaining that he is repaying part of his debts. Lopakhin wonders where Pishchik has got the money, and the old man explains that some English people have found a kind of white clay on his land. Handing another four hundred roubles to Liubov, Pishchik takes a drink of water. From a young man he has met on the train he has just learnt that 'some great philosopher or other . . . advises people to jump off roofs. You just jump off, he says, and that settles the whole problem.' Astonished at his own words, Pishchik asks for more water. Now he is off to pay some more debts, but on Thursday, Pishchik says, he will call again. Liubov points out that they are about to move, and that she will be going abroad the following day. Only now does Pishchik notice the piled-up furniture and the luggage, and he becomes tearful as he wishes them all every happiness. Having kissed Liubov's hand, Pishchik leaves, overcome by embarrassment, but he returns almost immediately, for he has forgotten to convey his daughter's greetings to the family.

Liubov says that they can leave now. Only two things worry her. One of them is Feers, who is ill; but Ania tells Liubov that Feers is in hospital. Liubov's other worry concerns Varia. Turning to Lopakhin, Liubov again speaks of her hopes that he and Varia might marry. Varia, Liubov claims, loves Lopakhin; and she herself cannot understand why the two of them seem to keep away from each other. Lopakhin replies that he is ready to settle the matter immediately, especially since he feels that he will never propose to Varia once Liubov has gone. Liubov finds the idea excellent, and Lopakhin points out that the champagne would come in handy too. Looking at the glasses, he realises that they are empty: Yasha has obviously been helping himself.

Left alone in the room, Lopakhin again glances at his watch. Varia eventually enters and starts examining the luggage, as if she were looking for something. Lopakhin and Varia exchange a few trivial comments related to her search. Varia goes on to explain that she has found a job as a housekeeper, and Lopakhin tells her that he will be going to Kharkov. He has engaged Yepihodov to look after the estate. Lopakhin then starts speaking of the weather, reminding Varia that the previous year it was snowing at this time. Varia makes little effort to reply. Eventually, a voice is heard outside, calling for Lopakhin, and he leaves the room immediately.

When Liubov re-enters, Varia is sitting on the floor, sobbing. Liubov reminds her that it is time to leave, and Varia stops crying and wipes her eyes. Confirming the failure of her meeting with Lopakhin, Varia says that she will be able to complete the journey to her new employer on the same day, provided that she does not miss the train.

Ania enters, followed by Gayev and Charlotta. Servants and coachmen come into the room, and Yepihodov attends to the luggage. Ania is happy that they are about to begin their journey. Gayev starts making a farewell speech, but Ania and Varia stop him, and Gayev returns to his billiard terms.

Trofimov comes in to announce that it is time to leave. Liubov wants to sit down for another minute: at this moment she is feeling as if she had never seen the walls and ceilings of the house before. Gayev remembers how, at the age of six, he watched his father through the window as he was going to church.

Lopakhin orders Yepihodov to check that all the luggage has been taken out. When Yepihodov replies in a husky voice and his new master asks the reason, Yepihodov explains that he must have swallowed something with the drink of water he has just had.

When they leave, Liubov says, there will not be a soul in the place. Completing her sentence, Lopakhin puts her right: 'Until the spring', he says.

Varia pulls an umbrella from a bundle of clothes, and Lopakhin pretends to be frightened that she may strike him with it.

Trofimov tells them that it is time to leave. Varia finally finds his goloshes, which she thinks look dirty and worn-out. As Trofimov again tells them to leave, Gayev's emotions are making him increasingly embarrassed.

Lopakhin checks that no one has been left behind and starts locking the doors.

Ania says goodbye to her old life and goes out with Trofimov. Varia leaves, followed by Yasha and Charlotta with her dog. Lopakhin goes out. Liubov and Gayev are left alone, and they embrace, sobbing quietly. Liubov takes farewell of the orchard.

Ania's happy voice is heard calling for Liubov, and Trofimov joins in her calls. Liubov looks at the nursery for the last time. Ania and Trofimov call again, and Liubov and Gayev leave.

The room is empty. There are the sounds of doors being locked and carriages driving off. In the stillness that follows, an axe thuds against a tree in the orchard.

Then there is the sound of footsteps, and Feers enters. He is looking ill. He walks up to one of the doors, tries it, and realises that he has been locked in the house. He sits down on a sofa, commenting that they have forgotten about him. He is worried about Gayev, who probably did not take his fur coat but left wearing only his light coat. 'These youngsters!', Feers sighs. He mutters, but then some words become discernible: 'My life's gone as if I'd never lived', he says. He lies down on the sofa, and remains motionless.

A distant sound is heard, like the sound of a string snapping. It slowly dies away, and silence follows, broken only by the sound of an axe striking a tree in the orchard.

NOTES AND GLOSSARY:

Vive la France!: (*French*) Long live France!

allez!: (*French*) go!

Holy Trinity day: in the Christian year, the Sunday after Whit Sunday

Part 3

Commentary

Dramatic technique

All four acts of *The Cherry Orchard* centre on social occasions. The great arrival in Act 1 is contrasted with the departure in Act 4, while the ball in Act 3 is set against the more informal gathering at the shrine in Act 2. As a result, quite a few members of the comparatively large cast tend to be on the stage at any one time. The playwright, furthermore, introduces all his characters early in the play, so that their individual features can emerge and their relationships develop without interference from new characters. Chekhov places his entire cast under the microscope, as it were, asking us to observe his characters' reactions to events and their interaction on the stage. And since the plot is so simple as to be almost predictable, it is the more profound implications of the characters' reactions and the overall effect of their interaction that are brought into the foreground. The technical aspects to be discussed here are all related to these special conditions and include Chekhov's means of characterisation, the qualities of the dialogue, and the use of action as a means of highlighting characters and character relationships. Finally, Chekhov's attention to structure and to the overall tone of the play will be considered.

Connected with each other by a network of parallels and contrasts, the characters in *The Cherry Orchard* form a distinctive group, and early in the play Chekhov alerts us to the significance of this group in a manner which is as bold as it is original. Defying any conventional rules about playwriting, he has a number of new characters, and major ones at that, walk on to the stage simultaneously, without having prepared us for their appearance. Liubov Andryeevna enters the nursery at the head of a procession of previously unseen figures, so that we are suddenly faced with no fewer than six new characters, who mingle with Lopakhin, Dooniasha, and several servants on the stage. We have had some advance information about Liubov, but we know nothing whatsoever about Ania, Charlotta, Varia, Gayev, and Simeonov-Pishchik. And as if this invasion of strangers were not sufficient to baffle us, Chekhov quickly has most of the characters walk out of the nursery. We are left with the impression of an arrival and a departure, a small-scale reflection of the overall rhythm of the action of the play.

Yet in this very short space of time, Chekhov has succeeded in giving all his new characters at least one speech each. These speeches all go some way towards characterising the speaker, and they also help to define the relationships between the characters. We learn that the middle-aged woman who is overcome with emotion on returning to her old nursery is the mother of the younger woman and the teenage girl. We are likely to be less certain about Liubov's relationship with the man whom she kisses several times, but we are bound to notice the sarcasm with which he comments on the efficiency of trains, and we may also hear in his words an echo of a comment made by Lopakhin at the opening of the play. The stout old man and the woman with the dog appear to be less closely related to the family group, but Chekhov neatly pairs them together, associating the woman with tricks and bringing out the old man's perpetual astonishment in the process. Taken together, these short exchanges also indicate the significance of form in *The Cherry Orchard*: Ania's, Varia's, and Liubov's joint enthusiasm for the familiar old rooms is set against Gayev's seemingly isolated comment about the train, which in turn is contrasted with Charlotta's and Pishchik's mutual interest in the diet of the dog. For all the differences between the topics of conversation, these speeches combine to create an overall rhythm, and distinctive patterns of character interaction are already beginning to emerge.

The characters, however, are not merely defined by their speeches: their costumes, appearance, and behaviour all contribute towards establishing both their individuality and their connections with each other. Chekhov was very conscious of these aspects of his characters, and his letters provide much information about how he envisaged his created figures on the stage.

In the section of the play under discussion here, we would undoubtedly be struck by Liubov's stylish way of dressing. The international cut of her clothes would contrast sharply with the traditional Russian outfit of Simeonov-Pishchik, for whom Chekhov prescribed 'a peasant's sleeveless coat . . . with heelless high boots', and with the nun-like costume of Varia, whose 'black dress with a broad belt' (Hingley, *The Oxford Chekhov*, III, 328) may well be glimpsed under her overcoat. Perhaps we would also discern a telling link between Liubov's appearance and that of Dooniasha, since the parlourmaid has previously been criticised for dressing herself up and doing her hair like a lady. The characters would be further defined by their various mannerisms. One of the most conspicuous would be Liubov's way of smiling. 'It's necessary to invent a smile and a way of smiling' (Hingley, *The Oxford Chekhov*, III, 327), Chekhov wrote when instructing Olga Knipper about the part of Liubov. In this section of the play, Liubov's smiling would combine with her tearfulness to give her character an aura of ambivalence likely to colour all our future impressions of her. We would also notice Ania's 'ringing voice' (Hingley, *The Oxford Chekhov*, III, 328). And somewhere in the background would be the figure of Lopakhin, with his distinctive way of moving about: 'he waves his arms about as he walks', Chekhov has explained, 'takes long strides and meditates while walking about – walking in a straight line' (Hingley, *The Oxford Chekhov*, III, 328). Gayev's striking manner of moving his arms and body *'as if he were playing billiards'* (Act 1) will subsequently reinforce the external similarities between himself and Lopakhin, thus creating a framework for the more far-reaching internal differences between the characters that the dramatic action will unveil.

Chekhov, then, uses speech, costume, appearance, and mannerisms to establish his characters and develop that network of contrasts and parallels which fuses them into a distinctive group. The methods as such are of course not original: the originality consists in the precision and economy with which they are employed, and in the complexity and subtlety of the effects which they produce.

The dialogue in the short section of the play which has been discussed here is marked by pauses as well as by some abrupt changes of topic. Features of this kind are typical of the dialogue in *The Cherry Orchard*, as are sudden stops, false starts, and silences. As has been indicated above (p. 37), these seemingly fragmented conversations tend to have a distinctive overall rhythm. Usually, they also have an inner logic, which is to be found at the level of thought and emotion. Here, this inner logic will be traced in a short exchange between Ania and Varia in Act 1.

When Varia, left alone with Ania soon after her arrival, suddenly abandons the topic of her expected wedding to Lopakhin and says, *'in a changed tone of voice'*, 'You've got a new brooch, a bee, isn't it?', Varia's instantaneous interest in Ania's new piece of jewellery is not as capricious as it may first appear. The change of subject is Varia's means of escaping from the fear and pain that accompany any talk about her relationship with Lopakhin. The change in her tone of voice betrays the fact that her interest is superficial: as is so often the case with Chekhov's characters, the speaker's thoughts are elsewhere. Ania's reply is no less complex. Speaking *'sadly'*, she explains that 'Mamma bought it for me'; but then she leaves Varia and goes into her room. When Ania continues, it is *'gaily, like a child'*: 'You know,' she says to Varia, 'I went up in a balloon in Paris!' Although Ania's initial sadness may to some extent re-echo the mood of her adopted sister, it is certainly not caused by the kind of feelings which are plaguing Varia: Ania is more likely to have been saddened by the memory of her mother squandering her non-existent money in Paris, wasting it on things like the bee brooch. At the same time, Ania cannot fail to be aware that the brooch is also a token of her mother's affection. Like Varia before her, Ania then drops a subject which is becoming too painful and difficult, rather as if she wanted to protect her sister. Ania controls her emotion by walking from the nursery into her own room. This change of environment appears to transform her, but it would be truer to say that she exploits it to feign a transformation: back in the room which has been hers since childhood, she pretends to be childishly delighted by her adventures in Paris, even to the extent of speaking about them with the gaiety of a child. In order to dispel the atmosphere of gloom, Ania reverts to her role of young and innocent girl. This, undoubtedly, is a role which her mother has wanted to continue to cultivate in her daughter, but it has been shattered by Ania's visit to Paris and her insight into the family's financial plight. In her reply, Varia reinforces Ania's role as a young girl. 'My darling's home again!', she exclaims; 'My precious girl!' With these words, Varia concludes their exchange in almost exactly the same way as it began, thus giving it a neatly rounded form. But although the words are almost the same, their implications are now quite different. At the end of the exchange, Varia is merely playing Ania's game, and it is only too obvious that both of them know that the innocence and simplicity of the past are gone for ever.

Throughout *The Cherry Orchard*, the dialogue has similar dimensions, involving several different levels of meaning. In particular, Chekhov has developed his dialogue into a superb instrument for recording clashing emotions within individual characters, one example being the contrast referred to above between Ania's adult sadness and childish delight. The character's tone of voice often betrays something of this clash. Significantly, Chekhov places a unique emphasis on directions for intonation: these abound in all his plays, but they are particularly frequent in *The Cherry Orchard*.* By modifying his characters' tone of voice, bringing their talk to a sudden halt, and having them switch, unexpectedly, to new topics, Chekhov is attempting to alert us to what is going on beneath the surface of the dialogue and within the various individuals involved.

As a means of reaching down to the level of submerged feelings, private memories, and associations which may not yet be fully accessible to words, Chekhov also uses clearly defined action. One conspicuous example, which involves repetition of this kind of action, centres on Varia and Lopakhin. Everybody is expecting the two of them to get married, but Chekhov, ironically, ensures that they become more closely associated with physical confrontation than with love and affection. When Lopakhin, in Act 1, puts his head through the door and bleats like a sheep, Varia clenches her fist, saying that 'I'd like to give him this . . .'; when Varia turns Yepihodov out of the drawing-room in

---

*See Nils Åke Nilsson, 'Intonation and rhythm in Chekhov's plays', in *Chekhov: A Collection of Critical Essays*, ed. Robert Louis Jackson, pp. 165–7.

Act 3 and swings Feers's stick, it is Lopakhin whom she very nearly hits; and in Act 4, after the failure of the proposal, Varia only has to pull an umbrella from a bundle of clothes for Lopakhin to react as if she were about to hit him. During the short spell when Varia is alone with Lopakhin, she pretends to be searching for something, and if the object she is looking for were the umbrella which she subsequently wields against Lopakhin, a nice comic touch would be added to their supposed tête-à-tête.

We are thus left with the image of impending confrontation as the paradoxical physical definition of the relationship between Varia and Lopakhin, but as always with Chekhov's writing, much is buried beneath the surface of the image. Varia's original desire to hit Lopakhin can partly be seen as a reflection of the frustration and ridicule she has suffered as a result of the stalemate in their relationship, but when she nearly hits him in Act 3, her desire is obviously about to be fulfilled rather too literally. This latter incident highlights the curious mixture of social expectation and private fear that characterises Varia's relationship with Lopakhin. On his part, Lopakhin inevitably sees Varia's behaviour in the context of his own experiences. The son of a serf, he has been beaten and thrashed throughout his childhood, and when Varia seems about to hit him with Feers's stick, she is not simply a woman whom he feels he has disappointed: she is also, and more importantly, one of those powerful superiors who have always resorted to physical force as a means of keeping him in his place. The irony of the situation is heightened by the fact that Lopakhin has just become the owner of the estate, thus effectively reversing the social relationship between Varia and himself. Varia's stick may not hurt Lopakhin physically, but it hits him mentally, spoiling his triumph with an unpleasant reminder of those social origins from which his money will never free him.

Another sequence of clearly defined action, the implications of which are worth considering, concerns Liubov and her treatment of the various telegrams she receives from her lover in Paris.

As has been indicated throughout this discussion of Chekhov's dramatic technique, the material of the play has been arranged and put together with a remarkable degree of care and sensitivity. Thus the potentially chaotic social occasion in Act 1 is constructed as meticulously as are any of the shorter sections which have been analysed above. With Dooniasha's and Lopakhin's initial meeting serving as a kind of prelude, Chekhov has arranged the remainder of the act in four parts. In each of these the problems of the family are considered, in a distinctive key and by a set of characters which is usually different from that involved in the previous part. Although the scene in the nursery may sometimes appear crowded and confused, with characters coming and going throughout the act and servants mingling with the central figures, the four parts stand out quite clearly. Thus the plight of the family is first discussed by Ania and Varia, and then expanded on and considered in more serious terms by Liubov, Gayev, and Lopakhin. As in a piece of music, a theme is introduced and then repeated in a more elaborate form. Part three represents a variation: Liubov and Gayev meditate on the beauty of the orchard through the open windows and delight in memories of their childhood, only to be reminded, by the appearance of Trofimov, of the irrevocable passing of time and the changed face of the present. In part four, finally, the theme is re-stated, varied, and rounded off as Gayev presents to Varia and Ania his plans for saving the estate. This part, then, echoes the first in that it involves Varia and Ania. Superficially, it differs from the previous parts in that it is pleasantly optimistic, but beneath Gayev's cheerfulness, hopelessness and despair are lurking.

The parallels with the structure of a piece of music hold good not only for the first act of *The Cherry Orchard* but for the play in its entirety. Large-scale elements and minute details are repeated and re-employed throughout the four acts, often with subtle but telling differences, so that the process of disintegration depicted in the action of the play is counteracted by the unifying rhythm of the carefully controlled and elegant artistic form which emerges. Thus the setting of the final act comes as an echo of that of the first, but with a change of key from major to minor as the nursery is about to be abandoned for good. In both acts, significantly, Lopakhin dominates the opening sequence, his somewhat mysterious presence in Act 1 foreshadowing his legitimate presence as the owner of the estate in Act 4. In the first act, too, we are introduced to Yepihodov's clumsiness, and when Lopakhin, immediately after his triumphant return in Act 3, bumps into a table and nearly knocks some candlesticks over, the parallel with Yepihodov's misfortunes adds a touch of irony which effectively undermines Lopakhin's new dignity. Further echoes are achieved by details such as Liubov's treatment of the telegrams she keeps receiving from Paris; by Feers's indefatigable and almost motherly concern for Gayev's well-being; by Pishchik's habit of falling asleep, snoring, and then waking up immediately, with a request for money on his lips; and by Yasha's contemptuous treatment of his mother, who waits as patiently for him in Act 4 as she had done in Act 1. The role of sound effects in the play helps to bring into focus the structural similarities with a piece of music, and it is significant that Chekhov, on several occasions, leaves the stage empty while concentrating the action of the play into a sequence of sounds. The most striking of these occurs at the end of the play, where the stage remains empty for some time while we are left to listen to the well-spaced sounds of doors being locked, carriages driving off, and an axe thudding against a tree in the orchard. The climax of this sequence is the re-iteration of the enigmatic sound of the breaking string, which at once rounds off Chekhov's work of art, confirming its affinity with a piece of music; and crystallises the issues of life and death which are at the heart of the playwright's preoccupations in *The Cherry Orchard*.

The tale of the loss of the estate is a sad one, but the overall tone of the play combines with the emphasis on artistic form to ensure that emotion is kept firmly in control. The advice which Chekhov once gave to a fellow writer of stories is pertinent here: 'When you depict sad or unlucky people, and want to touch the reader's heart,' he wrote, 'try to be colder – it gives their grief as it were a background, against which it stands out in greater relief.'* Chekhov is a master at achieving this coldness – which, it should be added, is in no way cynical or inhuman but perspicacious and even wise, stemming as it does from the author's profound insight into both man and art. In *The Cherry Orchard*, typically, situations are developed to the point where they become charged with emotion, only to be brusquely deflated, often in a manner which adds a touch of comedy. On Liubov's arrival, for example, her feelings overflow into tears and kisses – until Charlotta suddenly shifts both our attention and the mood of the scene by asserting, coldly and provocatively, that her dog actually eats nuts. Liubov's feelings are similarly checked as she speaks of her happy childhood while admiring the blossoming orchard – until Trofimov appears as an unpleasant reminder of the course her life has taken and of her present situation. A more complex example is provided by Gayev's presentation of his schemes for saving the estate towards the end of the act. Here it is not only the previous events that help to undermine the credibility of Gayev's optimistic words but first and foremost the situation of the speaker, who at this point is more anxious to comfort and encourage his young niece than to present a scrupulously truthful picture of the family's chances of retaining the estate. With their inherent ring of ambiguity, Gayev's words emerge as a neat illustration of the play's overall tone of controlled compassion and gently mocking irony, the irony in this particular case being directed towards the speaker himself.

Themes

'However boring my play may be,' Chekhov wrote of *The Cherry Orchard* in a letter to Olga Knipper, 'I think there's something new about it. Incidentally', he added, 'there's not a single pistol shot in the whole play' (Hingley, *The Oxford Chekhov*, III, 320).

It is true that the absence of pistol shots sets *The Cherry Orchard* apart from Chekhov's previous full-length plays: in *Ivanov* and *The Seagull*

*Letter to Madame Avilov, 19 March 1892, in *Letters*, ed. Friedland, p. 97.

there are suicides by shooting; in *Uncle Vanya* one character tries to shoot another but fails; and in *Three Sisters* one of the characters is killed in a duel. But although there is no violent death in *The Cherry Orchard* – indeed, no physical death at all – the entire dramatic action is overshadowed and moulded by the notion of impending death. Chekhov is exploring the condition of man, who is having to lead his turbulent life, so full of hope and expectation, of disappointment and bitter failure, in the knowledge that he is going to die and be reduced to dust. The condition of man is seen in the context of the cycle of life and death in nature, and Chekhov's overall emphasis on this fundamental pulse is crucial to the impact and meaning of *The Cherry Orchard*.

Here the themes of life and death will be traced firstly in the settings of the play, secondly in the plot, and thirdly in the private preoccupations of the characters.

Three of the four acts of *The Cherry Orchard* are set inside the old house belonging to Liubov Andryeevna, while the remaining act is set in the open, some distance away from the house. In each case, the season is an integral part of the setting, and as the spring of the first act turns into high summer, late summer, and, finally, autumn, the cycle of life and death is brought sharply into focus. The changing seasons are epitomised by the cherry orchard, and although the orchard can merely be glimpsed through the windows of the nursery, it thus emerges as a central element of the play's setting.

The play opens in the nursery, a room uniquely associated with the hopes and expectations of generations of Liubov's family. Dawn is breaking, and the emphasis on new and young life is further reinforced by the fact that it is a May morning, with the cherry trees in blossom outside the nursery. It is difficult to envisage a more perfect symbol of the triumph of life than the sea of delicate white blossom floating above the old tree trunks, and Liubov aptly expresses the sense of wonder the sight evokes: 'After the dark, stormy autumn and the cold winter, you are young and joyous again', she says of the orchard; 'the angels have not forsaken you' (Act 1). But the spectacle of the orchard in blossom is necessarily a short-lived one, and as if to remind us of the fragility and transience of this life, Chekhov has made the morning in Act 1 a cold one, with three degrees of frost in the orchard.

In Act 2, spring has turned into high summer; indeed, it is one of those warm evenings which make it a pleasure to remain out of doors although the sun is about to go down. The time of day combines with the details of the set – the ancient shrine, the stones which *'apparently served as gravestones in the past'* (Act 2), and the well – to create a solemn atmosphere, which further underlines the fact that this summer's evening marks a turning point in the cycle of life and death. The cycle has reached its peak, and from here it is possible both to survey the past and to gain some perspective on the future. Thus it is no accident that the setting opens up to reveal, beyond the centre-piece of shrine, stones, and well, '*the vague outlines of a large town*' (Act 2) on the horizon. While the ancient site in the foreground is closely associated with the estate and its people, the town on the horizon symbolises a new and different kind of life. Chekhov, then, enhances the significance of the cycle of life and death by indicating, on this summer's evening, that a social transformation is about to take place; and the line of telegraph poles becomes a conspicuous reminder that the estate is no longer a world of its own but an integral part of a rapidly developing society.

In sharp contrast to Act 2, Act 3 is set indoors. It is the evening of 22 August, the day of the auction. Unlike the other acts in the play, this act contains no direct references to the season, but the entire dramatic action is tinged with the melancholy that pervades the glory of late summer.

The set retains an echo of that of the previous act in that it has a distinctive perspective. But the perspective here, as we look from the drawing-room through the archway into the ballroom, is of the past and not of the future. In a letter to Stanislavsky, Chekhov stressed that

the house must be large and solid. Whether it's made of wood . . . or stone, that doesn't matter. It's very old and large. Summer holiday-makers don't rent that kind of house. That kind of house is usually pulled down and the material is used to build summer cottages. The furniture is old-fashioned, of good style and solid. The furniture and fittings haven't been affected by financial ruin and debts (Hingley, *The Oxford Chekhov*, III, 328).

With all the candles alight in the chandelier, the set has about it an air of splendour and festivity, but at the same time it is imbued with nostalgia. As Chekhov highlights the magnificence of the old rooms, we cannot fail to be conscious that the fate of the building is all but sealed, and that the ball we are witnessing is the last of the many which have been held there.

In the final act we are back where we began, in the nursery. Now, however, the curtains and pictures have been removed, so that the room, once the focal point of hope and expectation, conveys '*an oppressive sense of emptiness*' (Act 4). Never again will children grow up in the nursery, as Charlotta indicates with her final ventriloquist's trick, pretending to take farewell of a baby in swaddling clothes. Liubov, too, knows that the 'old grandfather house' is losing its inhabitants for good: 'Winter will pass, spring will come again, and then you won't be here any more, you'll be pulled down' (Act 4). From outside, the sound of an axe striking a tree has already been heard. There could be no clearer confirmation that we are witnessing not only the end of a growing season, but the end of an era.

Aptly, it is now October, with the morning chill penetrating into the old nursery: since the family is leaving, the stoves have not been lit. But all the details which, symbolically, spell death to the members of the family, are also shown to contain in them the seeds of new life. As in Act 1, the weather is sunny and calm, with three degrees of frost, and to Lopakhin this means 'good building weather' (Act 4). The cherry trees are being cut down, but in their place summer cottages will be put up, as a first step towards the future Lopakhin envisages: he feels certain that once the new occupants start cultivating their plots of land, Liubov's old orchard will be 'gay with life and wealth and luxury' (Act 1). The end of one era thus marks the beginning of another. The cycle of life and death will continue.

The plot of *The Cherry Orchard* is similarly moulded on the pattern of the cycle of life and death. The enthusiastic return of Liubov and Ania early in the play is of a piece with the optimism inspiring the various plans for keeping the estate within the family. Almost immediately, a special bond is established between the members of the family and the blossoming orchard, which becomes a symbol of that new beginning which is such a potent ideal, especially for Liubov and Ania. At the core of this ideal is the innocent happiness of childhood. Thus Ania, delighted to be back in her familiar surroundings, vows to run straight into the orchard as soon as she wakes up in the morning. And her mother, recalling her own childhood, speaks of how she 'used to sleep in this nursery; I used to look on to the orchard from here, and I woke up happy every morning' (Act 1). The hint of love affairs, within the triangle Dooniasha – Yasha – Yepihodov, and, more importantly, between Ania and Trofimov, adds to the atmosphere of youthful optimism and expectation.

The tone is already more sober and the situation less optimistic as the characters gather by the shrine and Lopakhin strives to impress on the members of the family the need for taking urgent action if they are to retain the estate. Liubov's and Gayev's failure to take heed of Lopakhin's warnings can be seen as characteristic of this particular stage of the cycle: half-way through the cycle of life and death the end is within sight, but as yet it does not appear sufficiently threatening to warrant any drastic action. In line with the details of the setting, the action also opens up perspectives on the situation of the family, ranging from Liubov's potted autobiography to Trofimov's survey of the social implications of the family's ownership of the estate. To his thinking, the orchard is a symbol of centuries of oppression. It is significant that Trofimov develops his views on the orchard in response to Ania's admiration of him: in this act, the love affairs are generally more heavily accentuated. But they are also shown to be more complicated than they first appeared, with some of the characters energetically denying the impact of the relationships in which they are so patently involved. On the evening of the day of the auction, not much hope remains. Varia is clinging to the possibility that her uncle has bought the estate with the money provided by Ania's grandmother, but Liubov knows only too well that the sum they have received is not large enough, and in the end she can only hope, desperately, that the auction never took place. In retrospect, the events of this entire act emerge in a cruelly ironic light, for when Gayev and Lopakhin eventually return, just before the end of the act, we learn that the auction was over by four o'clock in the afternoon. When Liubov greets her guests, she is thus in fact no longer the owner of the estate, and her hours of agony as she struggles to control her anxiety and keep up appearances are mercilessly prolonged for the most trivial of reasons: Gayev and Lopakhin have missed the train. In extreme compression, this is the situation of man, made all the more striking by a characteristically Chekhovian sense of irony: we are all facing the inevitable, and it is precisely this awareness of the end that imbues our lives and our ways of coping with the years allotted to us with such significance. This total and sometimes uncomfortable awareness also extends to the love affairs in this act, with Liubov forcing Trofimov to recognise his self-deception, while she herself acknowledges the full implications of her feelings for her lover by announcing that she will be returning to him.

The news of the sale of the estate has reached the family at the end of Act 3, and Chekhov uses the final act to elaborate on the consequences of this change, demonstrating how the cycle he has been tracing reaches down into death and then emerges to suggest a new beginning. In the final act, the hopes and expectations of the members of the family have finally been peeled away, and the characters are facing the stark reality of an empty nursery, from which only some items of luggage are waiting to be removed. No drama surrounds the members of the family any longer: the inevitable has happened, and all that remains for them is to leave the estate which has been their home for generations and go their separate ways.

Maintaining to the very end the ironic touch which has been noticeable throughout the play, Chekhov has Liubov claim that 'when we leave here there won't be a soul in the place' (Act 4) – only to make the family forget old Feers as the house is locked up. When the servant steps into the nursery to complete the play's great cycle of life and death, his new dignity is strikingly juxtaposed with his well-established comic role. Locked inside the cold, abandoned house, as if in a coffin, Feers surveys his existence and comes to the conclusion that 'my life's gone as if I'd never lived' (Act 4). The old servant is summing up an essential human experience, and all the main characters in *The Cherry Orchard* would recognise the truth of Feers's words. As he lies down, complaining that 'you haven't got any strength left, nothing's left, nothing' (Act 4), his death seems about to be enacted in front of our eyes, and it is only appropriate that he should remain lying motionless when the mysterious sound, as of a string breaking, and the sound of an axe striking a tree in the orchard are heard again. Through the character of Feers, Chekhov thus conveys the experience of death and its implications – and conveys them more vividly and dispassionately than he could have hoped to have done if he had depicted an actual physical death.

Although the action of *The Cherry Orchard* centres on the final months of the very long association between Liubov's family and the estate, it is thus not Liubov or even Gayev who enacts the death at the close of the play. Instead it is a former serf, a member of the social class in which Lopakhin has his roots, and which is now so directly involved in the transformation of society. Paradoxically, it is Feers's life-long resistance to change that opens up this perspective. The cherry orchard, for all its beauty, has been sullied by its dependence on serfdom; but it may well be the descendants of people like Feers who will lease the plots of land, build their summer cottages, and start growing vegetables, flowers, and fruit, thus bringing new life, and free life, to the ground where the orchard had once stood.

At the same time as the characters in *The Cherry Orchard* are involved in the plot sketched above, with its heavy emphasis on the cycle of life and death, they are also struggling with more private conflicts modelled on the same pattern. An illustration of these conflicts, and a partial explanation of their origin, are provided by Gayev's address to nature towards the end of the gathering by the shrine. 'Oh, glorious Nature,' Gayev begins, 'shining with eternal light, so beautiful, yet so indifferent to our fate . . . you, whom we call Mother, uniting in yourself both Life and Death, you live and you destroy . . .' (Act 2). Gayev never gets beyond this grandiose opening: as usual, his nieces force him to shut up. But he has already succeeded in defining an experience which is central to the characters in ˋChekhov's play, and both the elaborate form in which he puts it and the sudden disruption of his speech can be seen as symbolic expressions of the very point he is making.

Man is an integral part of nature's great cycle of life and death, with nature being just as indifferent to the fate of man as to the fate of the orchard. But unlike plants or animals, man has a consciousness which has the effect of setting him apart from the cycle of life and death. Nature may be indifferent to man, but the reverse certainly is not true: man is acutely aware of the brevity of his life-span and the inevitability of death. This awareness instils in him an urge to assert himself against the forces of nature, and this urge is manifested in his efforts to shape his existence in accordance with his own mind. All the characters in *The*

Cherry Orchard reveal an innate desire to impose some form and structure on reality before death blots out their identity, and Gayev's speech to nature is a case in point: with his unmistakable rhetoric, Gayev is putting his individual stamp on an observation which is a fundamental aspect of the condition of man. But the fact that Gayev is interrupted and his great design made to fall apart is just as significant as his efforts to formulate and structure his experience: the characters in *The Cherry Orchard* find themselves involved in a continuous struggle with forces that threaten to tear their creations apart. Gayev's disrupted speech thus illustrates both the desire for shape and the threat of destruction in a manner which is as neat as it is humorous.

Most of the characters in *The Cherry Orchard* have aspirations which reach further than those of Gayev in his speech: their concern with shape is not restricted to mere observations, but encompasses their entire lives. Chekhov's characters want to be in charge of their lives and determine for themselves the pattern of the years allotted to them. They set out, optimistically, when they are young and energetic, full of hopes and expectations, visions and magnificent plans, only to discover that the older they get, the more difficult it becomes to steer the course they had intended, and the more acute becomes the threat of disintegration. It is from this angle that Chekhov examines the condition of man in *The Cherry Orchard*, placing it against the backdrop of a distinctive cycle of life and death which only brings the contrasting energies of coherence and fragmentation more sharply into focus. The question which Chekhov ultimately is attempting to answer is this: is there a way of coping with life when we have to lead it not only in the knowledge that we shall die, but also in the shadow of our constant disappointment, and indeed despair, at the merciless progress of the forces of fragmentation?

With a range of different ages represented among the main characters in *The Cherry Orchard*, Chekhov can depict the various stages in an almost complete human life cycle. Ania is sufficiently young and inexperienced to retain most of her hopes and expectations intact, and she can face the world and the future with comparative confidence and optimism. Varia's attitude, although also that of a young person, is the opposite of that of Ania, for Varia has evolved a way of life which is an elaborate defence against the forces of fragmentation, her fear of the outside world having made her seek refuge in a nun-like existence on the estate. Against Varia's denial of the world stands Trofimov's extensive experience of it, but his grandiose visions of the future are undermined by his lack of self-knowledge and, indeed, by this perpetual student's entire way of life. Hard-working and realistic, Lopakhin appears to have a remarkable degree of control over his life; yet it is this character who is made to exclaim, at what should have been his moment of triumph: 'Oh, if only we could be done with all this, if only we could alter this distorted unhappy life somehow!' (Act 3). The forces which are wrecking Lopakhin's triumph stem from the collapse of his old friendship with Liubov, to whom uncontrollable forces of this kind are only too familiar: as a result of a series of personal tragedies, her life is in chaos. When she returns to Russia, it is in a desperate attempt to put together the shattered remains of her existence, but instead the process of disintegration is accelerated as Liubov is forced to realise that she cannot start her life afresh and that she no longer even has a home. The disintegration of Gayev's life is more advanced and more specific – he is said to have eaten up his entire fortune in sweets – and his chief remedies, speech-making and billiards, are not only appropriately constricted in their format but also suggestive of his fundamental impotence. The character of Simeonov-Pishchik, finally, is the epitome of disintegration, the old man's life being ruled entirely by his debts as he exists uncertainly from one repayment to the next. There could be no better illustration of the chaotic state of Pishchik's life than the short scene in Act 3 where he turns his pockets inside out in a desperate search for the sum he has just succeeded in borrowing towards his next repayment. Here Chekhov uses a classical comic device to make a serious point about the character of Pishchik, and with its striking ambiguity the small incident becomes profoundly revealing.

While the comedy of Pishchik's search through all his pockets has the air of being accidental, Charlotta deliberately produces effects of this kind and employs them as a means of coping with life. Charlotta is a strangely anonymous figure, who occupies a very limited space in the total action of the play; yet Chekhov insisted that Charlotta's was 'an important part' (Hingley, *The Oxford Chekhov*, III, 328). Charlotta differs from the other characters in *The Cherry Orchard* in that she is far less preoccupied with herself: with the exception of the opening of Act 2, she does not speak about herself but focuses her attention on entertaining her fellow characters with a variety of tricks. And these tricks, which Charlotta had learnt from her parents, are not used as haphazardly as we may first suppose: they emanate from a life marked by an unusual degree of self-knowledge and control, and their effect is always carefully calculated. The question-marks over Charlotta's background combine with her search for meaning in life and with her acute loneliness to confirm the essential fragmentation of human existence, but Charlotta's attitude points to a way of coping with this condition. Her tricks and performances serve as a means of controlling life, albeit temporarily, and giving shape and coherence to man's existence.

On a larger and more ambitious scale, Charlotta's performances are paralleled by those of the playwright, who is entertaining us all with his tricks on the stage. Through his work of art, Chekhov is enabling us to discern some of that coherence which life denies to so many of his characters, and as he shapes his material with a shrewd sense of humour, biting irony, and profound compassion, he is also, implicitly, indicating a possible attitude towards life. Chekhov is presenting human experience in a coherent, elegant, and deeply satisfying artistic form; and by doing so he is, in his own way, defying disintegration and death.

The characters

Liubov Andryeevna

'Nothing less than death can calm a woman like that', Chekhov once wrote of Liubov Andryeevna (Hingley, *The Oxford Chekhov*, III, 327). As we watch Liubov flitting about the stage in the opening act, talking, laughing, crying, and drinking coffee, we are bound not only to agree, but also to admire the insight, compassion, and precision which have gone into the creation of this vivid and convincing character. Liubov has a presence which completely dominates the company in which she appears in Act 1, and the character that is so strikingly established can soon be seen to epitomise the plight of other figures in the play, and, indeed, the situation of an entire section of society in an era of rapid and extensive change.

As Liubov switches from one topic of conversation to another, often giving the impression that her mood is just as adaptable, she may suggest to us that she is shallow and thoughtless. But these quick changes are better interpreted as reflections of her need for self-protection; and thus as parallels of the changes of topic and tone in the conversation between Ania and Varia analysed above (pp. 38–9). Just as Chekhov frequently deflates an emotional situation quite deliberately, Liubov can check her behaviour so that she appears, on occasion, to detach herself quite brusquely from her feelings. When Liubov first meets Trofimov, for example, she embraces him and cries at the memory of her dead son – only to regain her composure with a conscious effort: 'Ania's asleep there, and here I am, shouting and making a scene' (Act 1), she says, and proceeds to focus all her attention on Trofimov. In Act 3, where her anxiety is mounting as she awaits the return of Gayev and Lopakhin, she frequently seeks shelter behind her official role as hostess, thus making her behaviour seem one of extreme contrasts. But the woman who quarrels with Trofimov one minute and asks him to dance with her the next is not as fickle as she may appear: having spoken more frankly of her plight to Trofimov than to anyone else, she feels the need to cover up her painful admissions by returning to her official role. Conscious that she has hurt Trofimov, she is also anxious to ask his forgiveness. Liubov, then, is too complex a character and her suffering, despite her efforts, too palpable for us to write her off as shallow and thoughtless.

Liubov's character and situation both come more clearly into focus when she is seen in relation to her two daughters. In Ania, Liubov can recognise herself as a young girl, and it is no accident that Ania at one point is described as a kind of reincarnation of her mother: 'How like your mother you are!', Gayev says; and, turning to his sister, 'You looked exactly like her at her age, Liuba' (Act 1). Ania embodies all those hopes and expectations with which Liubov once set out in life, and this is no more apparent than in the final act, where Ania's enthusiasm jars with the mood of her mother. Varia, on the other hand, represents a projection of a very different alternative: serious, hard-working, and conscientious, Varia is in many respects the opposite of Liubov, but nevertheless she appears to share her adoptive mother's unhappiness and sense of profound frustration. The fate of Varia would suggest to Liubov that her own way of life is not to blame for her situation, but rather that they are both at the mercy of forces beyond their control. It is a sad but telling reflection of the general position of women in Chekhov's play that Liubov, despite her own experience of marriage, should be so keen on marrying off her daughters and continue to hope, right up to the very end, that Lopakhin will propose to Varia. In Liubov's fragmented world, the very institution of marriage remains a paradoxical guarantee of coherence and continuity; just how illusory this guarantee is, Liubov knows only too well.

Having lived her adult life first with her husband and then with her lover, Liubov is depicted, in *The Cherry Orchard*, without a partner. In view of the significance of men in her life, one dimension of Liubov may be taken to be missing from the play: we get no idea of those aspects of her which might emerge in the company of a man whom she loves. This missing dimension becomes all the more conspicuous as Liubov treats the men in the play with varying degrees of contempt. Simeonov-Pishchik is dismissed at an early stage, when he tries to steal the limelight by asking whether Liubov ate frogs in Paris and receives the answer that she ate crocodiles: Liubov obviously knows from experience how to silence Pishchik. As for Gayev, Liubov's brother, the happiness surrounding their reunion quickly gives way to open criticism by Liubov, whose cutting remarks about Gayev's efforts to borrow money and about his post at the bank show only too clearly what she thinks of him. Lopakhin, who declares soon after Liubov's arrival that he loves her 'as if you were my own sister . . . more than my own sister' (Act 1), goes on to alienate her with his proposal for saving the estate, and it is not long before Liubov is attacking him for his drab kind of life and the nonsense he talks. Trofimov retains Liubov's esteem longer than any of the other men, and to him she is noticeably outspoken, not only about the agony she feels during the ball, but also about the role of love in her life. Here Liubov treats Trofimov as if she were seeking in him a man who could truly share with her the pain she is experiencing, but inevitably, she is disappointed. 'You must say it differently... differently' (Act 3), she explains when Trofimov has answered her prayer for pity with a mere formal phrase; the difference she craves for is obviously that of his emotional involvement. When she goes on to criticise Trofimov for having neither a beard nor a mistress, she clearly is not just looking upon him as the prospective husband of her youngest daughter: she is being deliberately provocative, at a very personal level, in an attempt to test Trofimov's responses to herself. Trofimov confirms this dimension of their exchange by concluding it with the phrase that traditionally marks the end of a love affair: 'Everything's finished between us!' (Act 3), he says as he walks out to throw himself down the stairs.

Despite the formal reconciliation that follows, Trofimov has confirmed Liubov's essential loneliness. Her return to the estate and to her childhood nursery has been a thorough test of her situation, but all it has achieved is to open Liubov's eyes to the fact that the disintegration is accelerating. At the shrine in Act 2, Liubov ascribes her plight to her 'sins', but it is clear that Chekhov is not pronouncing any moral judgement on Liubov: she cannot be blamed for the course her life has taken. Liubov's assets in her middle-age crisis are first and foremost her self-knowledge, which enables her to face her situation without evasions; and, secondly, the dignity with which she learns to meet the collapse of her hopes. Liubov has less of this dignity at the end of Act 3, where she sinks into a chair in tears on hearing the news of Lopakhin's purchase of the estate, than she has at the end of Act 4, where she accepts the failure of her efforts to get Varia married to Lopakhin calmly and without any questions. Ultimately, Chekhov is indicating, it is only thanks to this self-knowledge and dignity that Liubov can rise above her fate.

Ania

Like her mother, Ania is at a crisis point in her life. She is the teenager about to break loose from her family in order to establish her independence, and this situation accounts for the contradictions in her behaviour: she is at once old enough to have an affair with Trofimov, whose visions of the future make a deep impression on her, and young enough to appreciate the shelter and security provided by her childhood nursery. Ania is just waking up to life, her encounter with Liubov's life in Paris being one of her most significant experiences so far, but she is still able to put aside and forget, at least temporarily, things which are unpleasant and painful. Before the first act is over, Ania has once more gone to sleep in the nursery, like the contented child she at least partly remains.

Ania is especially closely associated with her mother, and it is characteristic of the stage which the young girl has reached in her development that she alternately distances herself from the example of her mother and uses her as a model. Ania has been shocked and saddened by her mother's way of life in Paris, and she is openly critical of aspects such as Liubov's handling of money, but this does not prevent her from praising her mother for having gone abroad in the first place. 'Mamma couldn't bear it and went away', Ania says, referring to Liubov's personal tragedies; 'she never looked back.' 'How well I understand her!', Ania adds; 'if she only knew how I understand her!' (Act 1). The young girl is too inexperienced to realise that Liubov's return to the estate amounts to one great looking back, and it is significant that when she tries to comfort her mother after the sale of the estate she can only do so by looking to the future. But when Ania promises that Liubov's heart will one day be 'filled with happiness, like the sun in the evening' (Act 3), some of the enthusiasm already seems to have evaporated from her visions of the future, and it is difficult to imagine that her mother can feel truly convinced by her words.

The tempering of Ania's originally childish exuberance is largely the result of her relationship with Trofimov. There is a noticeable difference between the girl who enthuses about her old nursery in Act 1 and the young woman who dances with the student in Act 3. In between lie the crucial events at the shrine, where Ania's search for identity receives a new impetus and assumes a more clearly defined direction. Here Trofimov indicates to her the way ahead, his coherent, ideologically based concept of the future contrasting sharply with Ania's naive ideas; and as the girl walks down towards the river with the student, she can be seen to move into adulthood. At the end of the play, Ania and Trofimov seem about to be going their separate ways, yet it is on this couple that the hopes for the future are largely focused. While Liubov and Gayev take their painful farewells, Ania's happy calls from outside are echoed by those of Trofimov. The combination of contrasts and parallels connecting mother and daughter becomes an invitation to us to consider just how different Ania's life is likely to be – if at all.

Varia

While Ania's relationship with Trofimov helps to reinforce the similarities between the young girl and her mother, Varia's nun-like existence indicates just how anxious she is not to be seen to follow in the footsteps of her adoptive mother. The differences between Varia and

Liubov are physical and ideological and, perhaps most significantly, moral. The woman who is shocked by the idea of her younger sister travelling to Paris without a chaperon, and who checks the movements of Ania and Trofimov so painstakingly as to make herself ridiculous, clearly does not approve of her adoptive mother's way of life. Varia makes her position clear when she attempts to send away Lopakhin and Pishchik just as Liubov is about to have a cup of coffee with them soon after her arrival: social gatherings in the middle of the night are obviously not compatible with Varia's standards. Liubov dismisses her adopted daughter with a joke, but Varia demonstrates her displeasure by walking out of the room.

Against this background, we can hardly expect anything but a negative outcome of the final meeting between Varia and Lopakhin. Varia is not seriously interested in marrying Lopakhin, for he represents one of those dimensions of life which she has rejected for the safety of her nun-like existence. At first glance, her references to Lopakhin's expected proposal appear paradoxical as Varia goes on to declare that her greatest desire is to become a nun, but the contradiction highlights the confines of the way of life which Varia has evolved for herself. It is only logical that the man who makes her little world collapse by buying the property which has become her own private nunnery should also be the man whom everybody believes she is about to marry. Varia's manner of throwing down the keys on learning that Lopakhin has bought the estate indicates that the house matters more to her than any relationship with this man. Her preferences are confirmed in the final act, where she demonstrates her displeasure with the new owner by refusing to enter the nursery while he is present; when she is finally forced into the room, she does her best to pretend that she is searching for something and has not noticed Lopakhin. It is difficult to imagine a less auspicious prelude to a proposal.

Chekhov has described Varia as being 'a cry-baby by nature' (Hingley, *The Oxford Chekhov*, III, 326), and it is obvious that her frequent crying signals a sense of helplessness in the face of life. Varia cannot bear to listen to Ania's account of their mother's life in Paris; she is genuinely alarmed when Pishchik asks to borrow money from Liubov; and her encounter with the tramp sets her heart thumping. Varia's life is determined by fear of a kind that sometimes verges on cowardice, and this attitude contrasts sharply with the dignity displayed by Liubov. The character of Varia also illustrates just how impossible it is to impose any moral judgement on Liubov: the younger woman may be leading her life according to the strictest moral code, but she can only do so by shutting out the world, and thus she ends up dangerously ill-equipped to cope with the rather more demanding situation which changing circumstances are forcing her to face.

Gayev

With his speech-making, billiard terms, and compulsive eating of sweets, Gayev appears as an almost comically ineffective figure. His immaturity sometimes seems to verge on childishness, and this impression is reinforced by his dependence on Feers, who is permitted to treat Gayev as if he were still a little boy. But beneath this surface there is a fifty-one year old man who knows only too well that life has reduced him to a nonentity, singularly lacking in the esteem of others. Gayev, however, still has an innate urge to be seen in charge and in control of events. Thus it is Gayev who steps forward to direct the tramp in Act 2, and towards the end of Act 1, it is Gayev who sets out the various plans for borrowing money to save the estate. Responding, on this latter occasion, to Ania's sense of insecurity, Gayev can assume a role which adults normally deny him, and for a moment or two he revels in the reassurance of his own words.

Gayev's instinctive reaction to Ania's situation is in no way unique; rather, it is characteristic of this man, who is deeply sensitive beneath his layer of idiosyncrasies. An emotional person, Gayev easily finds himself embarrassed, and there is no mistaking his relief in the final act, when he and his relatives can eventually leave the estate which has cost them so much pain and suffering.

Against this background, Gayev's return from the auction need not be the almost shocking display of immaturity it may seem at first. Indeed, Gayev may even have equipped himself with his Kerch herrings quite deliberately, in an attempt to avert attention from the exceedingly painful subject of the auction. This manner of coping with difficulties is somewhat less dignified than that of Liubov; and it is significant that Gayev's eagerness to escape the tearful family gathering altogether makes him disregard any qualms about joining Yasha, his arch-enemy, in the billiard room.

Gayev's sensitivity, and more especially his manner of translating his impressions into words whenever he does not find himself overwhelmed by their sheer proportions and intensity, suggest that he is something of a failed poet. 'You haven't forgotten, Liuba?', he asks as he and his sister contemplate the beauty of the blossoming orchard. 'How straight this long avenue is – quite straight, just like a ribbon that's been stretched taut. It glitters on moonlit nights' (Act 1). For want of other means of giving shape and coherence to his existence, Gayev clings to words, thus providing occasional glimpses of the often painful acuteness with which he experiences life. When Gayev lands a job in a bank and ends up calling himself 'a financier' (Act 4) – a label which, incidentally, probably appears more pathetically ridiculous than Gayev is likely to realise – he is also, by implication, acknowledging the inadequacy of his world of words. As Liubov goes to Paris, Gayev goes to his job; and both of them are equally conscious of the fragility of their situations.

Lopakhin

Lopakhin's characteristics, attitudes, and outlook help to bring into focus that baffling passiveness and seemingly irresponsible detachment from reality which are eventually to cost Liubov and her family their estate. But Lopakhin is not just a foil to the other figures in the play; he is also a complex and satisfying dramatic character in his own right.

Coming as he does from a family which has worked its way up from the bottom layers of society, Lopakhin has learnt to equate life with work. It is hardly surprising that he should feel disorientated and even desperate in the company of Liubov and her family. Setting out on a business trip to Kharkov soon after four in the morning is no self-sacrifice to a man like Lopakhin, whose hands begin to feel strange as soon as he has nothing to do, and who reacts to Gayev's and Liubov's indifference to his plan for saving the estate by upbraiding them for being 'feckless, unbusiness-like, [and] queer' (Act 2). Lopakhin owes his position to the work of his ancestors and himself, and to him there are no limits to what can be achieved by work: by his standards, they all 'ought to be giants, living in such a country as this' (Act 2).

Lopakhin's devotion to work is coupled with a relentless realism and a ruthless honesty, with which he judges himself as well as others. Gayev, being an extreme contrast, comes into the firing-line more frequently than anybody else, as Lopakhin pounces on the inadequacy of his arrangements for borrowing money and even writes him off, albeit implicitly, as one of the many people in Russia who exist to no purpose. But Lopakhin gives credibility to these judgements by being no less honest about himself. He knows only too well that he shall never be able to escape from his peasant origins, and in front of Liubov he has no doubts about referring to himself as 'a fool and a half-wit' (Act 2), explaining that he has had virtually no education, and that his handwriting is such that he is ashamed of it.

Lopakhin's sincerity makes it impossible to look upon him as an evil, scheming capitalist: he is genuinely proud of his plan for saving the estate, and when he introduces it by claiming to want to 'tell you something nice, something jolly' (Act 1), there is no irony in his voice. Lopakhin is as incapable of anticipating the reaction to his plan as he is of understanding the family's failure to take action. His arduous climb from the bottom layers of society has not given him much opportunity to cultivate his sensibility, and this deficiency becomes conspicuous when Lopakhin is in the company of Liubov and her family. Characteristically, Lopakhin is the only one to put forward a cool and logical explanation of the mysterious sound that is heard towards the end of Act 2. Liubov, by contrast, is visibly upset, Ania gets tears in her eyes, and Gayev can only very tentatively suggest that the sound may have been caused by a bird, an idea which is also echoed by Trofimov. Lopakhin clearly lacks the perception which brings all the members of the family together as they feel the need to share their impressions of what is to them a hauntingly enigmatic, menacing, and even doom-laden sound. Thus the animosity between Lopakhin and Gayev must be seen as stemming, at least to some extent, from the puzzlement, incomprehension and defensive contempt which the insensitive person feels when confronted with someone who is in all respects his opposite. It is as significant as it is inevitable that Liubov's reaction to his purchase of the estate comes as a complete surprise to Lopakhin.

The attempted proposal in the final act perfectly defines that experience of personal loss and inadequacy which accompanies Lopakhin's triumph at the auction. Clearly upset by the collapse of his long-standing friendship with Liubov, Lopakhin agrees to the proposal in a final effort to please her; perhaps, too, he is anxious not to lose touch with the woman who once took pity on the poor, beaten son of a peasant. But the task to which Lopakhin agrees is one which demands an extreme degree of sensitivity and mutual understanding, and thus it is hardly surprising that Lopakhin and Varia end up conversing about the weather. What makes their inability to communicate less than comic is the fact that Lopakhin by now is at least aware that there are further dimensions to human existence than the concrete and practical aspects which have shaped his life so far. 'We show off in front of one another, and in the meantime life is slipping by' (Act 4), Lopakhin has recently said to Trofimov, thus indicating that he is gaining a new perspective on the condition of man and becoming conscious of man's need to express his inner experiences in an attempt to break his irrevocable isolation. Comic though it may appear, Lopakhin's failed proposal can thus be seen to encapsulate the tragic insight at the heart of the situation of Chekhov's characters in *The Cherry Orchard.*

Trofimov

Trofimov provides both a parallel and a contrast to the character of Lopakhin. Like Lopakhin, he is an outsider, who can take a critical view of the position of the family and relate it to a wider social context. But while Lopakhin is the practitioner, whose sphere is that of direct action, Trofimov is the theorist. His world is that of words.

The perspective provided by Trofimov is crucial to the ambivalence that comes to colour our judgement of both the family and the famous orchard. Up to the end of Act 2, the orchard is, among other things, a symbol of miraculous beauty and of the tenacity of life in a hostile climate, so closely associated with Liubov's family that it also becomes a symbol of family tradition and stability. But Trofimov adds a new dimension when he reminds Ania that her ancestors 'owned living souls' (Act 2). Once we have listened to Trofimov's words about 'human beings gazing at you from every cherry tree in [the] orchard, from every leaf and every tree-trunk' (Act 2), our mental image of the orchard is changed, and irrevocably so: the blossoming trees are no longer perfect in their beauty, for this beauty is dependent on generations of serfs, ruthlessly exploited by the owners of the orchard. Thus the situation of the family also becomes more complex than it may have appeared at first sight: its members are not the innocent victims of a sudden blow struck by the gods, but socially very privileged people who are guilty of failing to take account of the extent to which their way of life has depended on social exploitation.

Trofimov eloquently defines the ills of modern Russia, but both his devastating criticism and his magnificent visions of the future are undermined by his lack of self-knowledge and his own way of life. While the key word in Trofimov's gospel is 'work', he himself appears to be doing little effective work, and he does not hesitate to admit to Liubov that he expects to 'be a student to the end of my days' (Act 1). While claiming to be 'above love', Trofimov, towards the end of Act 2, is noticeably inspired by Ania, whose admiration and encouragement give a new fervour to his words and endow both his criticisms and his visions with a more specific and personal focus. Trofimov's childish behaviour in Act 3, where he reacts to Liubov's harsh but perceptive critique by staging what can only be interpreted as a mock suicide attempt, jars with the adult tone of his speeches, and the discrepancy is indicative of that lack of maturity and experience which is so fundamental to the student's zealous radicalism. It is also Trofimov's ideological simplicity that makes him respond to Liubov's pleas for sympathy by trampling her feelings in the dust on the day of the auction. In his failure to satisfy Liubov's need for understanding and compassion, Trofimov may thus appear to parallel Lopakhin, but there is an obvious difference: while Lopakhin simply is not equipped to perceive the significance of Liubov's inner world, Trofimov is clearly aware of it but chooses, for ideological reasons, to attempt to crush it. Ultimately, Trofimov's immaturity can make him inadequate to the point of cruelty when it comes to handling relationships with others.

In the final act, Chekhov is making fun of the proud ideologist as he has him spend most of the act looking for his goloshes: without them, Trofimov obviously cannot hope to make any progress at all towards the magnificent future of his visions. As he searches for his footwear among the luggage, Trofimov appears less cockily self-confident than in the previous acts, and this change seems to be borne out by his unexpectedly personal advice to Lopakhin, whom he tells to 'get rid of that habit of making wide, sweeping gestures' (Act 4), going on to compare Lopakhin's gestures to his optimistic talk of summer cottages growing up on the land of the estate. The most conspicuous verbal gestures in the play are of course those of Trofimov himself, and there is at least a possibility that the man who echoes Ania's happy calls from outside as the action draws to a close is now viewing both himself and the future in slightly more realistic terms.

Simeonov-Pishchik

Chekhov was remarkably sensitive to the ironies of life, and in the context of the plot of *The Cherry Orchard*, one of the functions of Simeonov-Pishchik is to bring out the irony of the fate of Liubov and her family. For all their struggle and suffering, the members of the family lose their estate, while Pishchik, who calmly sits back in the expectation that something will turn up, is miraculously saved by the discovery of a valuable white clay on his land. Pishchik is one of those happy-go-lucky people who seemingly undeservedly reach their goals and get what they want.

Pishchik is an obvious contrast to Trofimov and Lopakhin in that he has no understanding of their gospel of work. To Trofimov, the great visionary, Pishchik is a living illustration of the dangers of frittering away one's life on trifles, as the student emphasises when he criticises the old man for having wasted so much energy on finding the money to pay the interest on his debts: 'if all that energy had been used for something else', Trofimov points out, 'you'd probably have turned the world upside down by now' (Act 3). When Pishchik appears in the final act, not to borrow money but to pay some of his debts, he becomes an ironic question-mark in the margin of Lopakhin's achievement.

Throughout most of the play, Pishchik's situation parallels that of the family, but on a smaller scale, and in terms that are cruder and more extreme. As a result, Pishchik brings into focus features that are also to be found in the members of the family, although in less tangible form. They all share a fatalistic view of life, feeling that they themselves can do little to influence the course of events; and they are all egotistical, wrapping themselves up in their own plight to such an extent that they occasionally fail to respond to the situation of others altogether. In the case of Pishchik, this latter feature is a conspicuous one and the source of numerous comic effects. That the old man is living in a world of his own is apparent from the way in which he greets Lopakhin on his return from the auction; clearly, Pishchik is quite unaware of the implications of any news that Lopakhin might be bringing. Even more striking is

Pishchik's appearance in the final act, where he is so absorbed by the sudden upturn in his fortunes that he fails to notice that Liubov and her family are about to leave the estate for good, and has to have the situation pointed out to him by Liubov herself.

Although Pishchik's economic situation improves, there is clearly no change at the more personal level: he remains in a sheltered world of his own, where he no doubt will continue his irresponsible way of life to the end of his days. Pishchik knows nothing of that necessity for change and development which Trofimov preaches, nor does he share in Liubov's struggle for dignity and a degree of control over a chaotic existence. Yet we cannot write him off as morally reprehensible: Pishchik makes no secret of his need for the company and attention of others, and with all his shortcomings, he is so convincingly and familiarly human that we can only accept his approach as one out of many possible approaches to life.

Charlotta

For all the conspicuous differences in sex, age, and background, there are some striking parallels between Charlotta Ivanovna and Simeonov-Pishchik. The most obvious of these is their fondness for saying or doing something astonishing, which has the effect of suddenly making them the centre of attention, while the rest of the characters are relegated to the position of spectators. But while a trick such as Pishchik's swallowing of all Liubov's pills in Act 1 is done on an impulse, and is essentially an old man's rather clumsy attempt to ensure that he is not completely neglected, Charlotta's tricks are carefully planned and performed with a professionalism that reveals her total control, of her movements as well as of her life.

Charlotta Ivanovna has evolved a way of life which strikes the perfect balance. She is neither irresponsibly detached, like Pishchik, nor is she painfully involved, like Liubov. Yet she is as aware of the difficulties of coping with life as are any of the more patently perceptive characters in the play: it is no accident that it is Charlotta who poses the great questions about identity and meaning at the opening of Act 2, thus defining issues which are in fact relevant to all the characters in *The Cherry Orchard*. Perhaps as a result of her chequered background, Charlotta has found a way of facing up to these questions without permitting them to overwhelm her. Thus she is not in the slightest impressed when Yepihodov, albeit flippantly, threatens to commit suicide: killing oneself would clearly be a much too easy solution to Charlotta, and Liubov's suicide attempt in Paris would, by implication, leave her quite unperturbed. Charlotta's self-knowledge is not accompanied by self-pity.

Yet Charlotta is in no way insensitive to the plight of the characters around her. When her tricks become particularly abundant in Act 3, it is because Charlotta uses them as a means of assisting Liubov in entertaining her guests and keeping up appearances while the nervous tension mounts; for all the differences between the two women, Charlotta is obviously driven to act as she does by a deep sense of understanding and loyalty. At a more profound level, this commitment is reflected in the quality of some of her tricks, notably with the rug in Act 3 and with the bundle in Act 4. It is not cruelty and certainly not insensitivity that make Charlotta refer so directly to the plight of the family on these occasions: when she pretends to be auctioning a rug and then shows Ania or Varia to be standing behind it, or treats a bundle as if it were a small baby and then proceeds to take farewell of it, she is deliberately trying to distance the members of the family from their painful situation and so help them to cope with it. She is holding the mirror up to them, offering them an insight and a perspective akin to those which are provided by the playwright himself.

Yepihodov

Like all the figures in the service of the family, Yepihodov, the clerk on the estate, is more markedly comic than the main characters in *The Cherry Orchard*. In comparison with the characters discussed so far, the features and experiences of Yepihodov are both more extreme and more exaggerated. To take but one example, his misfortunes are not just abstract, like those affecting Liubov, but include calamities such as squeaky boots, flowers dropped on the floor, and repeated collisions with pieces of furniture.

Yepihodov's clumsiness is his most conspicuous characteristic, so well-known that he is commonly called 'two-and-twenty misfortunes' ('Simple Simon' would be a more idiomatic English rendering). This clumsiness also extends to Yepihodov's language, which is a strange jumble of phrases, no doubt picked up from his indiscriminate reading, which he believes singles him out as 'a cultured sort of fellow' (Act 2). When Yepihodov boasts about reading 'all sorts of extraordinary books', but then goes on to admit that 'somehow I can't seem to make out where I'm going, what it is I really want' (Act 2), he emerges as a hilarious but revealing parody of the intelligentsia as described by Trofimov later in the same act. It is of course no coincidence that it should be Yepihodov who crosses the stage in the background just as Lopakhin has declared that they all ought to be giants, living in a country like Russia: the appearance of Yepihodov at this very point confirms just how far they are from Lopakhin's goal.

Yepihodov is in love with Dooniasha, but, rather as we would expect, this is a disastrous affair, with the young girl responding to Yepihodov's advances by teasing him and making a fool of him. But for all the unmistakable comedy of Yepihodov's calamities, the pain they inflict on him is real enough, and his efforts to cope are as genuine as those of any of the main characters in the play. The man who feels that 'Fate, so to speak, treats me absolutely without mercy, just like a storm treats a small ship' (Act 2), is defining an experience which is just as relevant to Liubov Andryeevna, and all in all the clerk provides an effective comic gloss on the human plight at the centre of *The Cherry Orchard.*

Dooniasha

Against Yepihodov's comically exaggerated yet genuine efforts to cope with life stands Dooniasha's superficial approach. This superficiality becomes all the more conspicuous because Dooniasha models herself on Liubov. When the parlourmaid stares in her mirror, powders her nose, and claims to feel like fainting at the slightest excitement, she is, in her own eyes, faithfully reflecting the refined way of life of her mistress. Again, the contrast between Dooniasha and Yepihodov is significant: while Liubov's inner plight has a recognisable parallel in that of Yepihodov, Dooniasha's preoccupations add up to little more than a parody of Liubov's life. Dooniasha is too ignorant and imperceptive to be aware of her mistress's pain and suffering. The character of the parlourmaid thus has the effect of highlighting, by contrast, the complex inner life of Liubov herself.

This contrast extends to the area of relationships with men. To Dooniasha, this entire world is childishly simple and endlessly exciting, and she happily tells anybody who is willing to listen about the compliments she has received from her male friends. When Dooniasha tries to make Yasha promise to write to her from Paris, she is no doubt envisaging herself in the role of Liubov, getting a stream of exciting letters from her lover. One of the ironies, of course, is that Yasha will never implore Dooniasha to join him in Paris. But then Dooniasha will never comprehend the extent of the personal conflict which the telegrams addressed to Liubov have caused, just as she fails to discern anything of the emotional crisis which precedes Liubov's decision to return to her lover in Paris.

Dooniasha's existence exemplifies life on the surface.

Feers

With his disgruntled muttering and his habit of dismissing everything and everybody as 'daft', old Feers emerges as a distinctly comic figure. Chekhov also exploits his deafness for comic effects, making the old servant respond to orders which have never been given, and continue arguments in a vein which has already been abandoned. Feers's conservatism is so extreme that it frequently becomes comic too, and in this context his very appearance is significant: his old-fashioned servant's outfit reflects a formal meticulousness which is rendered comically irrelevant by the mounting plight of the family.

Feers, however, is not just a figure of fun: his idiosyncrasies contribute to highlighting aspects of the central characters and their situation. When Feers persists in treating the fifty-one year old Gayev as if he were still a little boy, or contemptuously refers to the emancipation of the serfs as 'the misfortune', he demonstrates a reluctance to face up to change and its implications which is also to be found among the members of the family. Feers's attitude to the emancipation is particularly conspicuous, since it concerns himself so directly: having been given the unique opportunity to live in freedom and determine for himself the course of his life, Feers has chosen to lead a life of dependence, not unlike the existence of generations of his ancestors. Feers prefers things to remain as they are, and his refusal to think independently and consider matters logically makes him the archetypal safeguard of the *status quo*. His outlook is not very different from that of Liubov and Gayev as exemplified by their reaction to Lopakhin's plan for saving the estate, and the social contrast between the old servant and the members of the family only helps to reinforce this similarity of attitude.

Feers's difficulties in taking part in conversations can also be seen to have a more profound significance. As the old servant struggles to grasp what has been said to him, and then continues his own line of thought, out of key with the conversation around him, he strikingly illustrates those problems of communication that are so typical of the characters in *The Cherry Orchard*. Like Feers, each of these characters is trapped in a world of his or her own and anxious to get through to others, but able to communicate only intermittently. The characters' awareness of the brevity of life and the approach of death can only add to the significance and urgency surrounding these efforts to communicate. The character of Feers neatly combines both these aspects, and as he speaks his final, broken sentences, he is defining experiences which are central to all the characters in Chekhov's play.

Yasha

Like Feers, Yasha is a man-servant, but the young man is doing his utmost to distance himself from the old man and all that he stands for. Not hesitating to tell Feers that it is about time that he went away and died, Yasha consistently treats Feers condescendingly, so as to make himself emerge in the best possible light. Having accompanied Liubov in France, Yasha is eager to appear as a man of the world, and he never misses an opportunity to stress the difference between himself and those employees on the estate whose fate it has been to remain at home. Dooniasha admires Yasha for being educated and able to reason about everything, but in doing so, she is only revealing her own ignorance and lack of experience: Yasha is merely showing off, and his efforts to seem superior rest on very shaky foundations. Yasha's method consists in seeking out those who are in any way weaker than himself, and then treating them with contempt, sometimes poking fun at them in the crudest manner. Mercilessly afflicted by misfortunes, Yepihodov is an obvious target for Yasha, who teases him, laughs at him, and jumps at the opportunity to make him appear ridiculous in public when the clerk breaks a billiard cue on the night of the ball. But the range of characters which Yasha can treat in this way is limited. His lack of discrimination is apparent from the fact that he makes repeated attempts to poke fun at Gayev, but Gayev retaliates, and the two of them become involved in a feud which lasts to the end of the play.

As Yasha uses ridicule and contempt to distance himself from the people employed on the estate, he inevitably reveals his own shortcomings. When he complains of their ignorance and lack of education, our attention is automatically drawn to Yasha's own ignorance and lack of education; and the ruthlessness with which he treats his mother shows that he is prepared to go to any lengths to safeguard the personal image which he is trying to create. Like Dooniasha, Yasha is an extreme contrast to the members of the family: disdaining any more profound emotional involvement, he exemplifies an approach to life which is no less superficial than that of the parlourmaid whom he treats so contemptuously.

Interpretations

'Stanislavsky has ruined my play' (Hingley, *The Oxford Chekhov*, III, 330), Chekhov complained to Olga Knipper not long after the première of *The Cherry Orchard*, and with Chekhov's claim begins an argument about the interpretation of the play that has continued ever since. In Chekhov's opinion, Stanislavsky had made his play excessively tearful, thus turning a work which the playwright himself had once described as 'a comedy, in places even a farce' (Hingley, *The Oxford Chekhov*, III, 319), into a sentimental tragedy. Chekhov, typically, was incensed to find that Act 4 with its farewell scenes was being dragged out for forty minutes: to his thinking it ought to last for a mere twelve minutes (Hingley, *The Oxford Chekhov*, III, 330).

Inevitably, interpretations of *The Cherry Orchard* have become coloured by the political and social upheavals which occurred in Russia little more than a decade after the completion of the play, and which, to some extent, appear to be foreshadowed in it. According to a recent Soviet interpretation, *The Cherry Orchard* is thus a satire on the old regime. Consequently, the plight of Liubov and most of the members of her family is trivial, while Ania emerges as a contrasting and crucially significant character, embodying the brighter future which the playwright indicates is lying ahead.* Conversely, a Western critic such as Maurice Valency has defended the 'blend of comedy and pathos' in Stanislavsky's original production.† In Valency's opinion, Chekhov's 'great talent lay in the sensitive depiction of the life around him, the physical and psychic landscape in which he lived'. But Valency is quite convinced that Chekhov had 'no theory of life to expound, no point to make, no thesis. It is quite unnecessary for the understanding of his drama to discuss his world-view. If he had anything of the sort, it was irrelevant to the subject of his art.'‡

A recent and interesting contrast to Valency's view is provided by John Tulloch's *Chekhov: A Structuralist Study*, Macmillan, London, 1980, in which *The Cherry Orchard* and other works are approached in the context of Chekhov's medical career and scientific values. But one of the best analyses of *The Cherry Orchard* as a work of art remains that of J. L. Styan in *Chekhov in Performance: A Commentary on the Major Plays*, Cambridge University Press, Cambridge, 1971; paperback edition, 1978. Styan's meticulous attention to detail and his sensitivity to Chekhov's dramatic and theatrical effects make his analysis at once faithful and elegant, perceptive and convincing.

*Harvey Pitcher, *The Chekhov Play: A New Interpretation*, Chatto & Windus, London, 1973, p. 163.
†Maurice Valency, *The Breaking String: The Plays of Anton Chekhov*, Oxford University Press, New York, 1966, p. 271.
‡*ibid.*, p. 184.

Part 4

Hints for study

General

When you first read *The Cherry Orchard*, it may well strike you as a confused and confusing play. This impression is likely to be due to a combination of factors: the comparatively large cast; the emphasis on conversation and small talk; and the simple, almost predictable line of the plot, which at times may make it seem as if little of significance is happening on the stage. Renewed readings will gradually reveal the role of the interaction between the characters in the play; the common themes, which pervade the separate conversations; and the elaborate form, of each of the acts and of the play as a whole, which has the effect of welding all the apparently disparate elements together into an artistic totality. This totality tends to become easier to perceive when the play is performed. Try to watch a performance of *The Cherry Orchard* if you have any opportunity to do so.

Since *The Cherry Orchard* is an unusually demanding play to read, you may find close study of separate sections of the play a convenient means of improving your grasp of it. Once you are familiar with the play and its characters, you may choose, for example, to look in detail at Act 2. This act begins in a low key, with only Charlotta, Yasha, Dooniasha, and Yepihodov present at the old shrine. Try to envisage the effect of the appearance and behaviour of these characters: there is Charlotta with her man's cap and her shot-gun; Yasha trying to look a man of the world as he smokes his cigar; Yepihodov, whom we already know as 'two-and-twenty misfortunes', playing his guitar; and Dooniasha incessantly staring in her mirror and powdering her nose. While one or two of these characters talk, the others are present on the stage and so contribute, silently, to the overall dramatic action. To take but one example, Charlotta's opening monologue is significant not just for what it contains, but also for the way in which it is received: drawing on her own experiences, Charlotta is making some crucial observations about the condition of man, and when her three listeners all fail to respond to her pleas for sympathy, they effectively confirm the truth of her words. As well as concentrating on the speaker, in this case Charlotta, the reader thus always has to remain aware of any other characters on the stage and of their role in the overall action of the play. Ultimately, this implicit relationship between the speaker and the other characters extends to *all* the other characters in the play, including those who happen to be absent. On this particular occasion, the central characters in the play have not yet arrived, but the experiences so unequivocally defined by Charlotta are obviously relevant to all of them.

In Act 2, the characters arrive on the stage in distinctive groups: Charlotta, Yasha, Dooniasha, and Yepihodov are followed by Liubov, Gayev, and Lopakhin; and finally Trofimov, Ania, and Varia turn up at the shrine. These well-spaced arrivals help to shape the act, creating three clearly defined sections which are connected by their themes. It is worth looking in detail at the ways in which the themes brought up in Charlotta's opening speech are reiterated and varied throughout the act, for example in Liubov's condensed autobiography, and in Trofimov's attacks on the state of Russia, especially as these are contrasted with his own existence as a perpetual student and 'moth-eaten gent'. More consistently and seriously than elsewhere in the play, the characters in this act are considering their situation, and considering it in the knowledge that they shall all have to die eventually. It is the accumulated effect of these preoccupations among the characters that creates the unique impact of the mysterious sound which is heard towards the end of the act. Most of the information about this unusual sound is to be found in a brief stage direction, which thus needs to be read carefully, as do all the other stage directions in the act. In particular, it is essential to establish a clear picture of the setting of the events in Act 2; for the tension between the ancient shrine in the foreground and the expanding town on the horizon adds significantly to the impact of the words spoken by the characters.

By reading the other acts in *The Cherry Orchard* with equally close attention, noting the parallels and contrasts linking them to each other, you will improve your understanding of the play and get a clearer idea of its overall form.

Study notes

You should start taking notes on the play as early as possible. By doing so, you can ensure that you are reading the play with attention; besides, you get into the habit of defining your impressions of it in writing. In preparation for a variety of examination questions, you need to take detailed notes on different aspects of the play, and to arrange these notes clearly and logically. Your notes on *The Cherry Orchard* could be arranged under headings such as 'dramatic technique', 'themes', and 'characters'. To this list you may want to add others, such as 'structure' and 'symbols'. Obviously, the questions which you have to answer at an examination may cut across these categories, but you may well find the basic headings useful for planning answers to any type of question.

Your notes under the heading 'themes' might be arranged along the following lines:

THE CYCLE OF LIFE AND DEATH

(a) *in the settings of the acts*:

Act 1: nursery, with orchard in blossom outside; spring; early morning

Act 2: in the open, with shrine, etc., and distant town; high summer; evening

Act 3: drawing-room and ballroom on the estate; August; evening on day of auction

Act 4: empty nursery; sunny but cold October day, 'good building weather' according to Lopakhin

(b) *in the plot*:

the initial, optimistic plans for retaining the estate, linked with Liubov's and Ania's enthusiastic return; desperate economic situation of family, combined with Liubov's and Gayev's inability to understand Lopakhin; hope evaporating on day of auction; end of an era as family moves out, accidentally leaving Feers, who enacts death while orchard is cut down outside. Possibility that descendants of serfs might build summer cottages and thus start new cycle of life and death

(c) *in the situation of individual characters*:

the cycle embodied in sequence Ania – Varia – Trofimov – Lopakhin – Liubov – Gayev – Simeonov-Pishchik; from youthful optimism (Ania) via mounting disintegration (Liubov) to total fragmentation (Pishchik); Charlotta as possible model, combining self-knowledge and acceptance of situation with degree of control and detachment, reflected in tricks and the ways in which they are employed

You will need to take separate notes on each of the main characters. Your notes on Liubov Andryeevna might be arranged as follows:

(a) *appearance and behaviour*:

style and elegance; smiling and tearful at the same time (return in Act 1); rapid changes of mood and topics of conversation (happy memories as she admires orchard in Act 1 – change with appearance of Trofimov – new change as she detaches herself from tragic memories)

(b) *life and present situation*:

potted autobiography in Act 2, combined with Gayev's comments on marriage and moral standards at end of Act 1; roles of Ania and Varia in throwing light on Liubov and her situation; her reasons for returning to estate; optimism in Act 1 set against growing irritation (with Gayev, Lopakhin) in Act 2; crisis during dance as she plays role

of hostess while awaiting news of auction, with Trofimov helping to
bring crisis into focus

(c) *Liubov's wider significance*:

crisis of middle-age epitomising universal human situation, with
growing awareness of approach of death; disintegration, but self-
knowledge and dignity as she learns to accept that she has neither
home nor country where she belongs

The sample notes above merely indicate how you might *arrange* your
notes, and for this reason examples backing up the various points have
been suggested only very briefly. When you take your own detailed
notes, you should include a range of examples, so that your arguments in
your answers to examination questions can be seen to be firmly based on
the text of the play.

Tackling examination questions

First of all, you should read the questions carefully and make sure that
you understand them properly. During an examination, this may be
more difficult than it sounds, and you may find that a special effort of
concentration is needed. When you have decided which questions to
answer, you should plan your time so that you can give each of the
questions the attention it requires.

When it comes to dealing with individual questions, you should
decide on the overall point you want to make, and then plan how to
make it logically, clearly, coherently and convincingly. Make up your
mind about which side to support in an argument, and ensure that your
answer is consistent throughout. Start putting your answer together by
jotting down words and phrases, thoughts and ideas which seem
relevant, and then arrange these to form the outline of your answer.
Make sure not to digress from your subject. Do not aim to fill the space
with summaries of the plot: normally, such summaries should be kept as
brief as possible, and should serve a purpose in your argument. Base
your answers on your own reading of the play, backing up your points
with well-chosen examples. The reading of criticism of the play may help
to clarify your ideas and may inspire you into making new discoveries in
the text, but remember that there is no substitute for your own detailed
knowledge of the play.

Try to plan your time so that you can read through your answers
before submitting your script. This should enable you to avoid some
unnecessary mistakes.

Specimen questions and answers

(1) 'It is around Lopakhin that the action moves.' (John Tulloch). Discuss.

If we interpret the word *action* in its everyday senses of 'process of acting', 'movement', 'exertion of energy or influence', it is true to say that the action in *The Cherry Orchard* moves around Lopakhin. Lopakhin reminds Liubov and her family of the approach of the auction; he puts forward a plan that will enable the family to retain the estate; he strives to alert the family to the mounting urgency of the situation; and he finally buys the estate, thus forcing the family to leave its ancestral home. Lopakhin is clearly the man of action in Chekhov's cast, and the very appearance and behaviour of this efficient businessman serve as constant reminders of his boundless energy. His manner of walking about, in a straight line and taking long strides, becomes a physical expression of the purposeful progress of his life: as a businessman and, subsequently, landowner, Lopakhin is continuing the social advance of his family, whose members, until quite recently, have been mere serfs. Lopakhin's habit of looking at his watch reflects his often impatient eagerness, thus neatly encapsulating the man of action in *The Cherry Orchard*.

But the impact of Lopakhin is also determined by the other characters in the play. Lopakhin emerges as the obvious man of action largely because his fellow characters are so remarkably passive. Liubov and Gayev fail to take Lopakhin's plan for saving the estate seriously, fail to heed his warnings, and so fail to retain their property. Trofimov preaches the gospel of work in terms which Lopakhin is bound to recognise, but then fails to live according to his words. And Simeonov-Pishchik, the play's most direct contrast to Lopakhin, does not work at all but merely sits back, waiting for something to turn up so that he can solve his most urgent financial problems. The character of Lopakhin is inextricably connected with these and other characters in the play, who form a unique group of created figures. If the word *action* is taken to mean 'the action of the play', that is, the series of events, great and small, which go to make up *The Cherry Orchard*, then it is not true to say that the action moves around Lopakhin. It moves, to an equal extent, around Liubov, Gayev, and all the other characters in the play. Paradoxically, much of the action of *The Cherry Orchard* centres on inaction, with many of the conflicts arising precisely because Lopakhin's energetic schemes clash with the attitudes of the members of the family. But if we are discussing the action of the play, it is this totality that we have to take into account.

Lopakhin is directly involved in the crisis surrounding the cherry orchard and, as the new owner, has his workmen start cutting it down. But the fate of the orchard is only the most tangible reflection of the complex conflicts experienced by the characters in the play. If the theme of *The Cherry Orchard* is defined in terms of the great issues of life and death, of identity and meaning, Lopakhin comes to belong on the fringe of the play rather than at its centre. *The Cherry Orchard* derives its pulse from the pattern of arrival and departure, and in this pattern Lopakhin has no place: it is embodied by Liubov and the members of her family. And while Lopakhin plans the future of the estate with untiring efficiency, Liubov and the characters around her are struggling with personal conflicts such as the accelerating disintegration of their lives and the inevitable approach of death. As a result of his background and way of life, Lopakhin lacks the sensitivity of Liubov and her family, and the great questions with which they are preoccupied have little relevance to him. It is true that he speaks with admiration of the sight of his one thousand acres of poppies, thus showing that he can appreciate beauty, but to Lopakhin the impact of these fields of flowers is directly related to his knowledge that he shall be able to make money from them. When Liubov and her family admire the blossoming orchard, it is in the knowledge that it is unproductive, but this in no way detracts from their appreciation. Lopakhin moves in a world where values are more concrete but also more superficial. His lack of sensitivity is reflected in his matter-of-fact reaction to the sound of the breaking string, which contrasts sharply with the sense of fear and doom it evokes in the members of the family. And although it is arguable that Lopakhin's experiences, notably the way in which his old friend Liubov receives the news of his purchase of the estate, help to sharpen his perception somewhat, the clumsy proposal scene with Varia makes it clear just how far removed he is from that inner world of intense and often painful feelings in which so many of his fellow characters dwell.

Only if we interpret *action* in its everyday sense, then, is it true to say that the action moves around Lopakhin. But the *action of a play* has a wider meaning, involving the total sequence of events, and seen in this perspective, Lopakhin is no longer the central figure in *The Cherry Orchard*. The character of Lopakhin is a distinctive creation, who helps to bring out crucial aspects of his fellow characters; but many of the conflicts which absorb them are obviously beyond his reach. Lopakhin gains his full significance as a member of a clearly defined group of created figures, to which he is connected by means of a network of contrasts and parallels. Ultimately, it is around this group that the action in *The Cherry Orchard* moves.

---

(2) How does Chekhov build up suspense in Act 3 of *The Cherry Orchard*?

When Act 3 opens it is evening, á band is playing, and Liubov Andryeevna's ballroom is full of dancing couples. It soon becomes apparent, however, that this is also the day of the auction, and that the hostess and her family are eagerly awaiting news of the outcome. 'The band came at the wrong time, and the party started at the wrong time', Liubov complains; but it is from this awkward combination of events that the tension which pervades the dramatic action derives. Beneath the surface of splendid entertainment, a drama is being enacted as Liubov and the members of her family are waiting to learn about the fate of the estate and of themselves.

As well as making tension an integral part of the situation in Act 3, Chekhov combines and contrasts his numerous characters and their individual preoccupations in a manner which heightens the suspense still further. More characters appear on the stage during this act than in any other act in *The Cherry Orchard*, and with all the comings and goings, the overall effect may initially be quite confusing. But the act is in fact very carefully constructed, with the character appearances juxtaposed in ways designed to create the maximum of suspense.

Liubov Andryeevna is both the owner of the threatened estate and the hostess at the dance, but Chekhov avoids focusing on her during the opening sections of the act. Instead, all the attention is directed to characters on the fringe of the main events. Having led the dance, Pishchik settles down and begins with Trofimov a conversation about the realities of his never-ending economic plight. When Liubov makes a brief appearance, characteristically singing a dance tune one moment and speaking of her anxiety the next, we may even feel that Chekhov is deliberately treating us to irrelevant details, especially as he insists on proceeding to focus on Charlotta and her tricks. From one point of view, these tricks are obviously mere entertainment, designed to divert the guests at the dance. The tricks, however, also epitomise the function of the dance itself, and when Charlotta's activities are combined with Pishchik's financial worries, which clearly reflect those of Liubov, it becomes obvious that this opening section is far more relevant to the central strand of events than it may at first appear. While being anxious like Pishchik, Liubov is having to entertain her guests in a way which is not very different from that of Charlotta. Chekhov thus heightens the suspense by refusing to focus on Liubov, preferring instead to reflect her complex situation via seemingly peripheral characters.

During the build-up to the central section of the act, a discussion between Liubov and Trofimov, tension mounts as the family's escape routes are seen to close one by one. Alone with Trofimov, Liubov temporarily abandons her official role and gives vent to her fears, but she also projects her situation on to the student. When Liubov speaks of fate driving Trofimov from one place to another, she is clearly referring to an experience which is also her own, and beneath her devastating attacks on him, we can sense her despair at her own situation. The tension is resolved when Trofimov throws himself down the stairs, but only briefly and ironically: as soon as it becomes apparent that his act has been a mere mock suicide, Liubov's genuine plight necessarily becomes more acute.

After Trofimov's mock suicide attempt, the pace of the action quickens, the growing sense of urgency adding to the mounting tension. In a final effort to re-establish the formal atmosphere of the dance, Chekhov has the station-master start reciting a poem, only to make the musicians interrupt him by striking up a waltz. The restlessness and impatience of the characters is becoming more directly reflected in their activities. Also, the servants are beginning to appear in the foreground, their presence pointing in the direction of a social upheaval, incompatible with the family's ownership of the estate. Thus attention is focused on Feers, who is not only criticising the social status of the guests but also complaining of feeling unwell; the old servant, furthermore, is supporting himself on a stick. Feers's words and appearance combine to suggest that matters are coming to a head. Soon after, Ania reports that a stranger has been heard saying that the estate has been sold. The tension mounts still further, especially as the stranger has disappeared without revealing any more details. Now there is a new urgency about the discussions and a striking frankness as the futures of Feers and Yasha are considered on the assumption that Liubov will have to leave the estate.

Although the dance is still in progress, the action centres on Dooniasha, Yasha, Feers, and Yepihodov. It is almost as if the servants had already taken over the estate, thus enacting the mounting fears of the members of the family. This, certainly, is how Varia sees it, and her quarrel with Yepihodov crystallises these anxieties. When she lifts her stick in order to keep him out, she is attempting to keep out those social classes which are threatening her established way of life.

The tension is partly resolved by the comic effect of Varia threatening Lopakhin with Feers's stick, but even after the businessman's arrival, it is a long time before the news of the sale of the estate is revealed. Here Chekhov is quite deliberately prolonging the wait by fitting in sequences such as Pishchik's incongruous reception of Lopakhin, and Gayev's arrival and comic departure for the billiard room. Only after the completion of this business does Lopakhin deliver the news, and the tension which has been mounting throughout the act – and, indeed, throughout the play – is finally resolved.

Chekhov, then, builds up suspense in this act by exploiting a situation which generates tension, and by arranging the events in such a manner that this tension grows, especially in the second half of the act. Using a range of well-known dramatic devices, such as locating the decisive events off-stage and introducing numerous delays and hold-ups, Chekhov has charged this act with tension to an extent that is unparalleled elsewhere in *The Cherry Orchard*. In doing so, he is entertaining us with his skills as a dramatist just as deliberately as Charlotta is entertaining her audiences with her tricks. The climax of this build-up is hardly meant to come as a total surprise; rather, the emphasis, as always in Chekhov's plays, is on the characters involved and their reactions to events.

---

(3) Write an essay about the symbolic function of the cherry orchard in Chekhov's play.

Chekhov's cherry orchard is one of the most famous symbols in world drama. It has a dual role which makes it uniquely relevant and satisfying, for as well as being the central symbol in the play, the orchard is also the focal point of the dramatic action. The conflict between Liubov's family and Lopakhin finds its clearest expression in their differing attitudes to the orchard, and the orchard becomes the means by which Trofimov can relate this conflict to a wider social context. Because of the role of the orchard in the action of the play, Chekhov is able to understress it visually, providing no more than a glimpse of the blossoming trees through the windows of the nursery in the opening act. The references and allusions in the subsequent acts succeed in conveying the more specific connotations of the central symbol without detracting from the magic that has come to surround it, and when we reach the final act, the mere sound of an axe striking a tree trunk is sufficient to communicate the fate of the orchard with all its implications – biological and individual, social and aesthetic.

In the first instance, the cherry orchard is a symbol of the changing seasons. The blossoming orchard outside the nursery in the opening act epitomises the miracle of spring, made all the more remarkable against the background of the long and hard Russian winter. The starlings that sing in the blossoming trees confirm this triumph of life, and as the members of the family admire the orchard, associating with it their happy memories and enthusiastic expectations, they are taking part in the celebration of life which the orchard embodies.

In the act set by the ancient shrine, the cherry orchard is virtually out of sight, but the extensive discussion of its fate combines with the powerfully evoked high-summer setting to conjure up a vivid image of the orchard at the peak of its biological year. As the family's hopes of retaining it fade away during the night of the dance, the decay brought by autumn can already be sensed in the late August air. In the frosty October morning of the final act, the new owner has taken charge of his property, and the sound of an axe striking a tree echoes through the nursery. The cherry trees have shed their leaves at the end of another growing season, but this time autumn is bringing a death that is final: the trees are being cut down to make way for summer cottages.

As a symbol of the changing seasons, the cherry orchard embodies the fundamental pulse of life and death. The reference to this pulse gives a unique significance to the orchard's symbolic functions in relation to individual characters, and to the society of which they are part.

The cherry orchard is most closely associated with Liubov Andryeevna, to whom its symbolic significance is first and foremost profoundly personal. The sight of the orchard evokes Liubov's childhood, when she used to sleep in the nursery and wake up 'happy every morning' (Act 1). But the orchard means more than this. 'All, all white! Oh, my orchard!', Liubov exclaims as she watches it. 'After the dark, stormy autumn and the cold winter, you are young and joyous again; the angels have not forsaken you! If only this burden could be taken from me, if only I could forget my past!' (Act 1). The miraculous rebirth of the orchard in spring becomes a reflection of Liubov's dream of starting afresh, and in this sense the blossoming orchard is of a piece with her spring-time return to Russia and to her ancestral home. The multitude of white blossom comes as a promise that it is possible and permissible to forget the past with all its pain, disappointment and despair, and to start anew with the innocence and optimism of the young child. Liubov's life has been a tragic and chaotic one, the deaths of her husband and her son followed by a spell abroad with a lover who has exploited her; but as long as the cherry trees blossom every spring, she dares hope for a change for the better. To such an extent does the cherry orchard embody Liubov's dream of a better, less fragmented life that she 'can't conceive life without the . . . orchard, and if it really has to be sold, then sell me with it' (Act 3). When Ania tries to comfort her mother after the auction, it is, significantly, with the promise of a new orchard: the young girl is perceptive enough to realise that in her cherry orchard, Liubov has been cultivating the kind of dreams which she needs to sustain her life.

In relation to Liubov, the wider social significance of the orchard is only implicit. The orchard, we learn, has become unproductive and is no longer economically viable, and in this sense it is a symbol of the entire social class which Liubov represents. As Liubov scatters her gold coins and gives them away, without even thinking as far ahead as the following day's dinner, she is enacting the bankruptcy of her social class, but without ever spelling out the parallels with the doomed orchard. By contrast, the social significance comes somewhat more clearly into focus in the case of Ania, whose relationship with Trofimov makes the orchard emerge in a new light. Initially, the role of the orchard in Ania's life has confirmed its purely personal symbolism: the childish enthusiasm with which Ania promises to run straight out into the orchard as soon as she has slept shows her to be a reincarnation of her mother, still in the midst of that innocent happiness which Liubov so nostalgically associates with the experience of waking up in the nursery and looking at the orchard outside. To Ania, then, the orchard is a symbol of happiness; but as a result of her relationship with Trofimov, her vision of happiness comes to extend beyond the confines of the orchard. From Trofimov, Ania learns of the family's perpetual debt to generations of serfs, and she realises that 'the house we live in hasn't really been ours for a long time' (Act 2). The orchard, too, is affected by these new insights. 'What have you done to me, Pyetia?', Ania asks the student. 'Why is it that I don't love the cherry orchard as I used to?' (Act 2). Ania's new awareness makes her distance herself both from her mother and from the narrowly personal symbolism of the cherry orchard. Yet Ania, with her combination of youthful exuberance and genuine innocence, retains a unique connection with the blossoming orchard, and it is no exaggeration to say that she continues to embody its spirit, long after its flowers have faded and its leaves begun to fall. 'Our new life is just beginning, Mamma!' (Act 4), Ania exclaims cheerfully as the family is about to leave the nursery for good, thus indicating that she is bringing with her out into the world some of that triumphant happiness and hopefulness which the blossoming orchard has symbolised.

The cherry orchard, as Gayev soberly points out, is mentioned in the Encyclopaedia, and it clearly also serves as the focal point of the family estate, the rows of old trees standing as living proof of stability and tradition. Feers, the eighty-seven year old servant, adds to this dimension of the orchard by bringing its past alive, speaking of the rich crops of cherries the trees used to produce, the various ways of preserving them, and the regular income the products would raise. Because Feers is a former serf, who has spent his entire life in the service of the family, the link between the personal and social significance of the orchard becomes very conspicuous. Feers conjures up a wonderful past, when dried cherries were sent by the cart-load to Moscow and Kharkov; and the dried cherries in those days, he assures his listeners, were 'soft, juicy, sweet, tasty . . .' (Act 1). This attractive image of the past is of a piece with the general outlook of the old servant, to whom the emancipation of the serfs is still 'the misfortune', and who has refused to avail himself of the opportunity to become a free man. To Feers, then, the orchard is a symbol of the good old days, and there is no contradiction between his happy memories and his own social position. But with even the recipe for drying the cherries having disappeared, the era which Feers glorifies is obviously gone for ever, and the servant, aged and increasingly ill, emerges as a confirmation of the precariousness of the family's situation. Feers may still be able to conjure up images of the productive orchard of the past, but the orchard with which he becomes most directly identified is the bare and doomed one of the final act. While young Ania embodies the spirit of the blossoming orchard in spring-time, the old servant who is left behind in the empty house becomes a personification of the trees awaiting the axe in the autumn morning.

Unlike Liubov, Ania, and Feers, Trofimov sees the symbolic significance of the orchard chiefly in social terms; and to him any personal significance is strongly coloured by his ideological outlook. Uppermost in Trofimov's mind is the fact that the serf-owners who were Ania's ancestors 'owned living souls', and to the student these generations of serfs have become inextricably bound up with the orchard: 'Don't you see human beings gazing at you from every cherry tree in your orchard, from every leaf and tree-trunk, don't you hear voices?', he asks Ania (Act 2). Trofimov urges Ania to free herself from the sullied property of her family. Yet when he speaks to her of the marvellous future of his visions, it is, significantly, the image of the orchard that he uses to communicate the scope and quality of his dreams. 'The whole of Russia is our orchard' (Act 2), he assures her. Trofimov makes no secret of his disapproval of Liubov's orchard; yet, like her, he needs an orchard in which to cultivate his dreams. Trofimov's dreams are the products of his political convictions, but when he resorts to the image of the orchard to put them across, he gives them a special power and impact, infusing them with the life and beauty of the blossoming cherry trees.

Lopakhin, by contrast, envisages a future in which there is no place for the orchard. In his opinion the trees should be cut down so that the land, which is close both to the town and the railway, can be divided into plots for summer cottages. But although Lopakhin's plan would entail the destruction of the orchard in which so many characters, notably the members of Liubov's family, are cultivating their memories and expectations, his scheme is not to be seen as a deliberate, evil plot against the family. To the self-made businessman, the plan to cut down the trees and build cottages on the land is the perfect solution to the family's financial problems, and when Lopakhin puts forward his ideas, he is quite unaware of the extent to which he is offending Liubov and Gayev. Lopakhin is the descendant of serfs on the estate, and his concept of the orchard leaves no space for the appreciation of beauty for its own sake: to him it is a simple matter of using the land to the best advantage, just as the men who had owned his ancestors would have ensured that they were exploited as efficiently as possible. To Lopakhin, then, the significance of the orchard is social and economic. But even so the orchard – or rather, the site of it – remains the focal point of his dreams for the future, just as it nourishes the hopes of so many others in the play.

The cherry orchard, then, has a different symbolic significance for each of these characters, with Chekhov covering a scale that ranges from the purely personal symbol to the purely social one. Yet to all these characters – Liubov, Ania, Feers, Trofimov, and Lopakhin – the orchard symbolises some of their most cherished ideals. To Liubov it promises a new beginning; to Ania it means youthful happiness; to Feers it is a reminder of the good old days; to Trofimov it is a metaphor for his grandiose vision of the future; and to Lopakhin it is the perfect site to develop so as to attract the people who can give it a new lease of life. The cherry orchard becomes a latter-day Garden of Eden in which all these characters can cultivate their hopes and beliefs. And with the orchard being so closely linked with the cycle of life and death, the role of these hopes and beliefs is brought more clearly into focus: they are part of the mental sustenance which man requires for his survival. Ultimately, then, there is also an aesthetic dimension to the symbolism of the cherry orchard. For all the daring optimism of Lopakhin's plans, the world without the cherry orchard is going to be a poorer place, with less scope for beautiful hopes and memories. It seems no accident that the substance which unexpectedly saves Simeonov-Pishchik from financial ruin is a clay that is white, like the orchard in blossom. Pishchik's clay comes as a sober reminder of the miracle of the reborn orchard in the opening act. The clay yields money, as Pishchik proves by handing over bundles of notes to Lopakhin and Liubov; but it is a heavy, clinging substance, buried, moreover, in the ground. For all its profitability, Pishchik's clay lacks utterly the palpable life and inspiring beauty of the orchard, and it is clearly not going to nourish the hopes and memories of women and men in the way that the orchard has done. It is a bleaker and more prosaic future which begins to open up as we listen to the sound of the axe in the final act of *The Cherry Orchard*.

Some further specimen questions

Questions on the characters
(1) Compare and contrast the characters of Trofimov and Lopakhin.
(2) Do you agree with Maurice Valency's claim that Liubov's failure to take action to save the estate is due to the fact that 'she herself is full of guilt, and greatly desires to suffer'?
(3) In what ways do the servants in *The Cherry Orchard* illuminate the central characters?

(4) 'Chekhov's great achievement is to put the important stress on *relationships between* characters rather than on the characters themselves' (J. L. Styan). Discuss, with reference to *The Cherry Orchard.*

Questions on the dramatic technique
(1) Compare and contrast the structure of the first and last acts of *The Cherry Orchard.*
(2) Analyse the techniques which Chekhov uses to establish the character of Gayev, and evaluate the effects he achieves.
(3) Write an essay about Liubov's treatment of the telegrams she receives from Paris, showing how her reactions help to illuminate her character and her changing situation.
(4) Analyse the proposal scene between Lopakhin and Varia in Act 4 in the light of Harvey Pitcher's claim that 'what is remarkable about the scene is the complete lack of importance of the words themselves. They are being used not to convey meaning, but as emotional messengers, and the pauses and dots in the text are of much greater significance.'

Questions on themes and symbols
(1) Analyse the role of the changing seasons in *The Cherry Orchard.*
(2) Write an essay about the main themes in Act 2 of *The Cherry Orchard.*
(3) Consider the extent to which Lopakhin's words in Act 3, 'Oh, if only we could be done with all this, if only we could alter this distorted unhappy life somehow!' reflect central themes in the play.
(4) Do you agree with the claim that 'the real symbolism of the loss of the cherry orchard [is] the destruction of beauty by those who are blind to it' (Ernest Simmons)?

Part 5

Suggestions for further reading

Biography

SIMMONS, ERNEST J.: *Chekhov: A Biography*, Cape, London, 1963. The most comprehensive biography of Chekhov.

HINGLEY, RONALD: *A New Life of Anton Chekhov*, Oxford University Press, London, 1976. A somewhat shorter study. Contains an appendix on 'Chekhov in English', which covers imaginative works, letters, and biographical and critical studies.

Letters

FRIEDLAND, LOUIS S. (ED.): *Letters on the Short Story, the Drama and other Literary Topics by Anton Chekhov*, Vision Press, London, 1965. A useful collection. For other collections, see the appendix to Hingley's biography.

Criticism

STYAN, J. L.: *Chekhov in Performance: A Commentary on the Major Plays*, Cambridge University Press, Cambridge, 1971. A detailed and sensitive analysis. Contains photographs of the first production at the Moscow Art Theatre.

The author of these notes

HELENA FORSÅS-SCOTT was educated at the University of Gothenburg, Sweden, and the University of Aberdeen, Scotland. She has taught in the Department of Scandinavian Languages at the University of Gothenburg and in the Department of Scandinavian Studies at the University of Aberdeen. She has contributed articles, mainly on Swedish novelists, to *Swedish Books*, and an essay by her on John Arden's play *Serjeant Musgrave's Dance* is due to appear in *Modern Drama*. She is currently working on a book about the plays of John Arden, and on an English language anthology of texts by Swedish women writers.